What Works! Successful Writing Strategies for National Board Certification

What Works! Successful Writing Strategies for National Board Certification

Third Edition

Bobbie Faulkner

BLOOMSBURY ACADEMIC
NEW YORK • LONDON • OXFORD • NEW DELHI • SYDNEY

BLOOMSBURY ACADEMIC

Bloomsbury Publishing Inc, 1359 Broadway, New York, NY 10018, USA
Bloomsbury Publishing Plc, 50 Bedford Square, London, WC1B 3DP, UK
Bloomsbury Publishing Ireland, 29 Earlsfort Terrace, Dublin 2, D02 AY28, Ireland

BLOOMSBURY, BLOOMSBURY ACADEMIC and the Diana logo are trademarks of Bloomsbury Publishing Plc

First published in the United States of America 2026

Copyright © Bloomsbury Publishing Inc, 2026

Cover image: istock/Olga Yastremska

All rights reserved. No part of this publication may be: i) reproduced or transmitted in any form, electronic or mechanical, including photocopying, recording or by means of any information storage or retrieval system without prior permission in writing from the publishers; or ii) used or reproduced in any way for the training, development or operation of artificial intelligence (AI) technologies, including generative AI technologies. The rights holders expressly reserve this publication from the text and data mining exception as per Article 4(3) of the Digital Single Market Directive (EU) 2019/790.

Bloomsbury Publishing Inc does not have any control over, or responsibility for, any third-party websites referred to or in this book. All internet addresses given in this book were correct at the time of going to press. The author and publisher regret any inconvenience caused if addresses have changed or sites have ceased to exist, but can accept no responsibility for any such changes.

A catalog record for this book is available from the Library of Congress

ISBN: HB: 978-1-4758-7516-4
PB: 978-1-4758-7517-1
ePDF: 978-1-4758-7518-8
eBook: 979-8-7651-5504-2

Typeset by Deanta Global Publishing Services, Chennai, India
Printed and bound in the United States of America

For product safety related questions contact productsafety@bloomsbury.com.

To find out more about our authors and books visit www.bloomsbury.com and sign up for our newsletters.

Contents

Preface vii
Acknowledgments viii

Introduction 1

1 What Is National Board Certification? 3

2 Building Your Foundation 7

3 Getting Started and Getting Support 13

4 The Reflective Teacher, Metacognition, and the National Board Process 21

5 Writing for the National Board 25

6 Probing the Prompts 41

7 Component 2: Differentiation and Writing About Student Work 51

8 Writing for Component 3: The Video Component 63

9 Writing for Component 4: Effective and Reflective Practitioner 83

10 Component 1 Writing at the Assessment Center 91

11 Candidate Care 101

12 Confusing Topics and FAQs 109

Appendix A: Ten Commandments for Survival as a National Board Candidate 115

Appendix B: Ten Editing Tips to Trim Space without Trimming Content 117

Appendix C: Sentence Stems for Analytic and Reflective Writing 118

Appendix D: Component 3: Analysis of a Video 119

Appendix E: Video Tips for Component 3 120

Appendix F: SSTARS Lesson Plan Template Based on the Architecture of Accomplished Teaching 122

Appendix G: Twenty Tips from Component 4 Assessors 123

Appendix H: Component 4 Section Connections 125

About the Author 126

Preface

The National Board Certification process is now in its third "generation" of development. In Generation 1.0, the process consisted of six entries covering the gamut of classroom instruction and professional development, and a full day of content-based, constructed response(essay)-type, Assessment Center exercises. Next, came Generation 2.0, with four entries (some parts of Generation 1 were combined) and a continuation of the six Assessment Center Exercises. Between 2014 and 2017, the National Board revised the process for a third time, to create Generation 3.0, which is the current process as of the printing of this book in 2021. Generation 3.0 consists of four components covering Differentiation in Instruction, Classroom Environment, Assessment, and Professional Development. The Assessment Center Exercises are now a mix of the traditional Constructed Response items and a Selected Response (multiple choice) section.

Consistent through all versions of the process, from its inception in the 1990s to the present, is the need for writing that is clear, consistent, and convincing. The scoring rubrics for each component are based on those writing qualities. The intention of this book is to give National Board candidates a toolbox of writing strategies that will pave the path toward certification. Here's wishing you the very best on your National Board journey!

Acknowledgments

I would like to offer heartfelt thanks to those who have contributed to my National Board journey. From Scottsdale, I owe appreciation to Nancy Gallagher Creighton, former Career Ladder specialist whose open mind and dedication to teachers allowed National Board Certification to take root and grow in Scottsdale. I also owe thanks to the core group of Scottsdale Candidate Support Providers, Susan Leonard, Mary Zongolowicz, Tammy Andreas, and Abbey Bobbett who have been instrumental in promoting and growing the program. The National Board candidates I've worked with along the way have been both a professional and personal inspiration. A personal thanks goes to my husband, Jim, who has encouraged me all along the way and tolerated my many hours in front of the computer. Finally, the staff of the National Board itself deserves recognition for being unfailingly supportive of National Board Candidates, especially in the school years when Covid-19 turned everyone's teaching world upside down.

Introduction

This book began with one of those off-the-cuff remarks that no one dreamed would ever actually amount to anything. "You ought to write a book," a fellow facilitator said one day after we finished a workshop for National Board candidates. And that's what I did. This book is an update of the original *What Works! Successful Writing Strategies for National Board Certification* published in 2014.

This book is meant to be a practical, user-friendly resource for candidates in all certificate areas. The information contained in its chapters reflects my own experience as a candidate and facilitator of candidates, the study of the National Board process, and the needs and frustrations of actual candidates.

This book is a supplement to the comprehensive body of information and instructions provided to candidates from the National Board for Professional Teaching Standards (NBPTS). Information contained in the official NBPTS documents always trumps any other source, including this book.

Successful Writing Strategies contains tips, information, documents, and examples that have been created solely for the purposes of demonstration and are neither approved nor endorsed by the NBPTS. Please keep the following in mind as you read:

- The author is not a trained assessor and does not imply that any samples in the book would score well or lead to certification according to the NBPTS scoring rubrics.
- Writing samples are fabricated and not from actual candidate writing.
- Writing samples are for demonstration purposes only and may not reflect all guidelines suggested by the NBPTS. They cannot be copied or used for submission.
- *Successful Writing Strategies* is as accurate and current as I could make it. Be aware that NB information is periodically updated and requirements do change over time. It is the responsibility of the candidate to be informed of the current NBPTS requirements.

Successful Writing Strategies is a labor of love for my fellow educators and National Board candidates. It's my hope that this book will make your journey to National Board Certification just a little easier.

1 What Is National Board Certification?

Six Word Memoir: Know your standards: know them well!
BRITNEY: NC

NBPTS Background and History

National Board Certification is a national *voluntary* system that certifies teachers who meet a set of high and rigorous standards for what accomplished teachers should know and be able to do. This certification system was developed by the National Board for Professional Teaching Standards (NBPTS) and put in place in 1987 following recommendations from the Carnegie reports *A Nation at Risk* and *A Nation Prepared*.

The National Board has developed high, rigorous, research-based standards to measure the effectiveness of a teacher's practice. The process involves an extensive series of performance-based assessments that include teaching portfolios, student work samples, written commentaries, videos, thorough analysis of the teacher's classroom practice and the impact on student learning. In addition, teachers complete a series of written exercises that probe their depth of knowledge of their subject matter.

The work is based on long-established research that identifies and recognizes sound educational practices that result in student learning. The NBPTS has commissioned more than 140 studies and papers on the value of the certification process as well as its standards and assessment. The process has also been validated by a number of independent studies.

The Five Core Propositions

The Core Propositions are the heart of the National Board process. They outline the expectations and values for what *accomplished* teachers should know and be able to do, and are the umbrella under which the other elements of the National Board Certification process are organized. Accomplished teaching implies going *above and beyond* what is typically expected of the average teacher. The Propositions describe skills in the following areas:

- **Proposition 1: Commitment to Students**

    Accomplished teachers know the developmental levels of their students, believe all students can learn regardless of background, and use their knowledge to design effective instruction for all students and a variety of learning styles.

- **Proposition 2: Knowledge of Subject**

    Building upon their knowledge of students, accomplished teachers advance their own understanding of their content area and develop a wide range of strategies to set high and worthwhile goals to teach that subject matter to their students.

- **Proposition 3: Manage and Monitor Student Learning**

    Accomplished teachers understand how to manage, motivate, monitor, and assess student learning by planning appropriate learning sequences to achieve the desired outcomes and adjusting instruction as needed. Accomplished teachers also know how to structure the learning environment for optimum learning.

- **Proposition 4: Think Systematically about Their Teaching and Learn from Experience**

    Accomplished teachers analyze student learning and reflect on their teaching practice. They then determine the next set of high and worthwhile goals, implement appropriate instruction, and continue the analysis and reflection cycle.

- **Proposition 5: Teachers Are Members of Learning Communities**

    Accomplished teachers collaborate with other professionals, parents, and their larger community to support and enhance student learning.

The Standards

There are twenty-five certificates that cover many subject areas and student development levels. Each contains a set of Standards, which, along with the

Five Core Propositions, form the foundation of National Board Certification. The Standards identify specific knowledge, skills, and attitudes that support accomplished practice, while emphasizing the holistic nature of teaching. They identify how a teacher's professional judgment is reflected in action and they reflect the Five Core Propositions.

To achieve National Board Certification and be considered an accomplished teacher, a candidate must show *clear, convincing, and consistent* evidence that *his or her teaching practice reflects the standards*. Understanding the standards and how to demonstrate them in practice provides evidence of accomplished teaching.

What Works! Understanding Your Standards

- Read the standards multiple times. Pay attention to the examples included in each.
- Think about how you already incorporate the standards.
- Highlight things you already do regularly in one color, things you do sometimes in a second color, and things you rarely or never do in a third color. This will help you recognize your strengths and what might be bolstered in your practice.
- Show clear, consistent, convincing evidence that your teaching is based on the standards.

Why This Works! The standards were developed to identify accomplished teaching. Candidates are expected to show evidence of the standards within their teaching.

The Process

National Board Certification is a rigorous process that may take up to three years to achieve. Candidates are asked to:

- Demonstrate within their teaching practice the rigorous standards discussed above.
- Show leadership, collaboration, learning, reflective practice, and professionalism.

- Prepare a portfolio of three written components that document your teaching practice.
- Focus on the analysis of student work samples, classroom practice and professional development, collaboration and leadership.
- Make videotapes of the teacher working with his/her class.
- Complete a series of subject-specific written tests at an Assessment Center to document knowledge of their subject area.

National Board Certification is the highest, most comprehensive voluntary professional development experience available to teachers. Examining their teaching practice and professional accomplishments in depth provides teachers a professional growth experience unlike any other.

2 Building Your Foundation

Six Word Memoir: Architecture is the backbone of lessons.
RUSSELL, VT

Who Is an Accomplished Teacher?

In a nutshell, an accomplished teacher is one who goes *above and beyond* what is typically expected. Accomplished teachers practice exceptional, skilled teaching. They have a strong knowledge base of subject matter and pedagogy, demonstrate complex, nuanced professional work, and consistently meet rigorous standards of practice. Accomplished teachers are committed to their students, know their subjects and how to teach them, know how to manage and monitor student learning, reflect on their practice and learn from their experience, and are learners, collaborators, and leaders within their professional communities (the five Core Propositions).

Accomplished teachers are teachers just like you, who try their best every day to meet their students' needs, keep current with pedagogy and subject knowledge, and work with others in their schools and districts to create an environment conducive to supporting the healthy growth and development of their students academically, socially, and emotionally.

What Is Accomplished Teaching?

Accomplished teaching is the double helix of knowing your subject and how to teach it. The two strands are tightly entwined and seamlessly connected. Accomplished teaching combines both the art and craft of teaching along with a solid knowledge base of content and child development.

Accomplished teaching means planning and demonstrating effective instruction for *these students, at this time, in this place*. The National Board describes accomplished teaching practices in the Standards developed for each certificate. They are specific teaching behaviors that accomplished teachers demonstrate within their teaching practice. As a candidate for National Board Certification, you will show evidence of the standards in your teaching practice.

The Architecture of Accomplished Teaching (AAT)

The *Architecture of Accomplished Teaching (AAT)* is a double helix representation of accomplished teaching practice as it applies to the lessons candidates use in their components and in assessment center exercises. It is designed to give a "visual" of how the accomplished teaching of units of study and lessons are organized. It is an under-used tool that can add greatly to the understanding of the National Board process and what the National Board is "looking for." Candidates often lament that if they just knew what the National Board "wanted," they'd know what to do for each component. In truth, candidates who understand the Architecture of Accomplished Teaching and use its structure as the basis for planning their lesson sequences will demonstrate what the assessors "want"—evidence of accomplished teaching. This tool is found in your *Portfolio Instructions Part 1*. Keep a copy near your computer for frequent and easy reference.

What Works! Studying the Architecture of Accomplished Teaching

Step 1 - Start with knowledge of your students *(Proposition 1)*

- Who are they? Where are they now in their learning? Where should you begin?
- What knowledge about your students influenced the goals you set?
- How do you incorporate this knowledge into your lesson planning?

Step 2 - Continue setting high, worthwhile goals *(Proposition 1)*

- How do the goals you set connect to your standards and portfolio instructions?
- How do the goals fit into the sequence of your overarching goals?

- What do you want your students to know at the end of the lesson or unit?

Step 3 - Implement instruction *(Proposition)*

- What approaches do you plan to use to accomplish your goals?
- In what sequence might you plan the strategies you plan to use?
- How will the strategies you choose support your students learning?
- What is your rationale for implementing instruction this way?
- What criteria might you use to decide if and when to use another strategy?

Step 4 - Evaluate student learning *(Proposition)*

- How will you assess student learning?
- Why did you choose these methods for these students at this time, in this setting?
- What evidence will let you know the instruction was successful or not?
- What, if anything, did the assessment(s) tell you about your instruction?
- Where will you go next?

Step 5 - Reflect on the effectiveness of your lesson design and decisions *(Proposition 4)*

- How do you know whether you made the right choices?
- What was successful and what was not?
- How could students reflect on their own learning?

Step 6 - Set new, high, worthwhile goals *(Proposition 4)*

- How will you decide when it is time to move on in the lesson sequence?
- What indicators will you use to set new goals?

SSTARS: Here is an acronym to jog your memory about the AAT.

- **S**tudents: Know your students and how they learn. (Proposition 1)
- **S**et high, worthwhile, and appropriate goals. (Propositions 1 and 2)

- *T*each using appropriate, effective strategies. (Propositions 2 and 3)
- *A*ssess student progress using a variety of evaluation types and forms. (Proposition 3)
- *R*eflect on your teaching and your students' progress. (Proposition 4)
- *S*tart the process again.
- See the Appendix for a lesson plan template using SSTARS.

Why This Works!

The elements of the Architecture of Accomplished Teaching provide a complete lesson/unit plan that will have the greatest impact on student learning.

What Works! Knowing When to Use the Writing Styles.

- Use mainly *descriptive* writing with some analysis for Steps 1, 2, and 3.
- Use mainly *analytical* writing for Step 4.
- Use mainly *analytical and reflective* writing for Steps 5 and 6.

Why It Works!

Use the Architecture of Accomplished Teaching to discern the nuances in the prompts. This will help you use the appropriate writing style for each. The prompts align with the Architecture's steps and using it will help you find evidence of your thinking and teaching to write about.

The Scoring Rubrics

The Scoring Rubrics found in the Scoring Guide and at the end of each component are also underutilized resources that can be life-savers. This is the document assessors have beside them as they score. How your component will be scored is not a secret! Everything you need to show evidence of is listed in a user-friendly bullet format in the Scoring Rubrics.

What Works! Studying the Rubrics

- Read all of the levels from Level 4 down to Level 1. You will see a great difference in the quality of evidence present in each one.
- Concentrate on the Level 4 Rubric. Keep it beside you as you write so you'll know exactly what evidence you need to show. Be sure you have evidence for each bullet. Notice how it aligns with parts of the Architecture of Accomplished Teaching. Use the Level 4 Rubric to self-assess each component. Go through it bullet by bullet to ensure you've included everything you need. If something is missing, put it in!
- A great many candidates score in the 2 and 3 family. Notice the more nuanced differences that occur between these score families.

What Works! Include the 3-Cs of Evidence:

- *Clear:* Anyone who reads your written commentary should be able to understand what you are saying. You've explained acronyms and educational terms. The sequence of events can be easily followed. Your writing is readable and makes sense.
- *Consistent:* Your writing needs an element of continuity. Don't say one thing in the first paragraph, and then contradict it later. Numbers must add up, timelines need to be accurate and your data shared honestly.
- *Convincing:* Present the case that you are an accomplished teacher. This means you present your evidence, and it is believable and achievable. The best way to do this is to include specific examples, documentation, and verification. Including specific examples provides stronger, more convincing evidence.

Why It Works!

Using effective tools such as the Architecture of Accomplished Teaching, the Scoring Rubrics, and Evaluation of Evidence Guide will make the process less frustrating and more meaningful, because you'll know where to go for guidance and clarification. Make these tools work for you!

3 Getting Started and Getting Support

Six Word Memoir: Start sooner NOW, rather than later.
LYNN - AZ

Learning the Standards, the Lingo, and the Component Requirements.

New candidates often don't know where to start. They know they're embarking on a unique journey, but aren't sure what steps to take first. If this describes you, read on.

- Refresh your understanding of the Five Core Propositions. They are the umbrella under which all other National Board documents are organized.
- Read and internalize the standards for your certificate. You must know what they look like in practice, and how you use them in your practice.
- Read the General Portfolio Instructions document. This is an underutilized resource with wealth of information that is easy to refer to later.
- Study the *Learning Portfolio-Related Terms* (GLOSSARY) section to become familiar with National Board "language" that is specialized and specific to the National Board process. Learn to read it, understand it, and write it. Certain phrases are used repeatedly in your instructions, and the glossary is where they are defined.
- Familiarize yourself with the component *Overviews* at the beginning of each set of Instructions to understand the content of each component.
- Study the *What Do I Need to Do?* section of each component for a list of requirements.

What Works!

Familiarizing yourself with component requirements, National Board "language" and resources will give you the tools and confidence to move forward.

Organize Your National Board Materials

Once you have a basic overview of the portfolio, it's time to implement some organizational strategies to help keep the myriad of Written Commentary drafts, paper piles, and artifacts you'll assemble. Here are several systems candidates have used successfully. Pick one or a combination that suits your own style and work habits.

What Works! Organizational Options

- Spiral-bind each set of component instructions as well as your certificate standards. You'll end up with a "book" for each component that is easy to carry and reference. They're also sturdy and will stand up to heavy use. Your school may have a machine that does this operation or go to an office supply store.
  - Keep instructions in a large binder sectioned for each component. This keeps all instructions in one place and it's a familiar and easily managed organizational system.
  - Invest in a file box with sections or use hanging folders. Designate folders for each component, including student work, assessments and data.

Why It Works!

Following a **KISS** System (**K**eep **I**t **S**uper **S**imple) will be a lifesaver. You won't stress over the time wasted hunting for lost work. Remember to designate a place for your work—and keep it there always! Knowing where to go quickly for information will save you time and grief and enable you to work smart!

What Works! Organizing Your Written Commentary/Documents on Your Computer

- Get comfortable with your computer—it will become your best friend.
- Figure out how to bookmark documents from the NB website and your work so you can access them quickly and easily.
- Use a reliable word processing program such as Word or Google Docs.
- Follow all instructions as to font, type size, line spacing, margins, headers, and footers.
- Label each draft with the date. This will assure you are working on the latest version.
- Create a folder for each component and save drafts in their appropriate place.
- Periodically print out drafts or back them up on a CD or flash drive/memory stick you can use on any computer. This step will save you a lot of stress if your computer crashes or your laptop is lost or stolen. You can also email drafts to yourself on another computer.
- Remember: save early, save often, and save everything! Back up your files frequently.

Why It Works!

Doing everything you can to keep your writing accessible and safe is prudent. Nothing would be worse than losing what you've worked so hard to produce!

What Works! Organizing Your Time

Figuring out how to organize your time is by far the most difficult challenge. Family and work continually compete for your time and energy. Following are some strategies successful candidates have used to help them cope with the time demands pursuing National Board Certification places on them:

- Say no at school! Eliminate as many committees and school responsibilities as possible. Promise your principal you'll be back next year.

- Say no at home too. For this school year, delegate chores and activities. This is not the year to become team parent for all of your kids' sports teams. Resign if you already are . . . spread the joy and let some other mom or dad take a turn.

- Set aside a designated daily or weekly work/writing period. Some candidates arrange for their spouse to be in charge of the family on Saturday or Sunday afternoon, or for one weeknight. Other candidates stay late at school once a week or go to their classroom to work on the weekend.

- Consider arranging a weekend now and then away from home so you can work undisturbed. Go to a hotel, a friend's cabin, or anywhere you can be alone.

- Recognize that in the spring you'll need additional time to finish and polish entries.

- Create a flexible, realistic timeline and do your best to stick to it. Your timeline will be determined by the number of components you plan to complete within a school year.

- Avoid procrastination; it will come back to haunt you. Some teachers say they work better under pressure, and that may be true at times. But in the National Board process you can't quickly dash off a paper and produce quality components. The components require a great quantity of quality evidence collected over time, and putting together a successful product is too complex to be done in a hurry.

- Be aware you will likely need to work on more than one component at a time, especially if you are completing all four components in a single year.

- Use your academic scope and sequence to map out units for your components.

- Look at each component and earmark lessons you teach that will fulfill the requirements.

- Research terms/processes you aren't familiar with. For example, Component 4 requires a Formative Assessment, three Student Self-Assessments, and a Summative Assessment. If you are unsure of the purpose and use of any of these, do your homework ahead of time.

  - *Save* everything. Save student work. Save evidence of anything that could be used for the Participation in Learning Communities section of Component 4.

Why It Works!

Organizing your time wisely can be a make-or-break factor in the quality of your component submissions.

Build a Support System: Cohort Support

When National Board Certification began, candidates were few and far between both in numbers and location. It wasn't unusual for someone to be the only candidate in their entire state. Fortunately, today few candidates face that kind of isolation. Thanks to National Board Certified Teachers who have certified in the past, a continuum of support has developed across the country. Candidate support systems may be available in or near your school district within university communities and State agencies. Candidate support is designed to foster your professional development as you work through the Certification process.

If you are in a cohort, you will work with a Candidate Support Provider (CSP) /Professional Learning Facilitator (PLF) who will guide your group and be obligated to provide and uphold ethical candidate support according to NBPTS guidelines.

CSP/FLP Responsibilities:

- Help candidates think more clearly and deeply about their teaching practices.
- Help candidates learn to analyze the evidence presented. Help candidates engage in self-evaluation.
- Offer patience and encouragement.
- Guide candidates toward making their own decisions about evidence.
- Meet regularly with the candidate cohort and encourage peer collaboration.
- Share knowledge, skills, and experiences.
- Listen nonjudgmentally.
- Ask probing questions.
- Maintain confidentiality.

A CSP/FLP cannot:

- Guarantee any particular score, especially a certifying score.
- Tell candidates that something is wrong, flawed, not good enough, or that a component will or will not score well.
- Make a judgment call about component instructions that seem unclear.
- Share NBCT components or videos that have been submitted as examples or tools.
- "Make" candidates into accomplished teachers or a National Board Certified Teacher.
- Create evidence for candidates or tell them how to write the Written Commentary.
- Tell candidates which students to feature, which student work to submit, which videos to submit, or which segment of a video "will work."

If you participate in a cohort, you have responsibilities too . . . both to yourself and to the group.

Candidates' Responsibilities:

- Make an investment in time and attend scheduled meetings.
- Share fears, concerns, and issues.
- Continually read, review, and apply the NB Standards.
- Bring work and questions to sessions.
- Keep to established timelines.
- Accept feedback in a professional manner.
- Study the component instructions.
- Come to meetings prepared.
- Maintain confidentiality.
- Commit time to the process.
- Celebrate steps along the way.

What Works!

If you don't have a cohort, you can still find support. Try these ideas:

- Form your own cohort. If there are other candidates in your district or area, organize a monthly meeting. Consider rotating the location so all candidates host the group.
- Find online support. There are many Facebook pages devoted to National Board Candidates. Some are geared to service candidates from any certificate area, while others are certificate area-specific.

Why These Work!

Collaborating with others gives you a sounding board and a place to ask questions and hear others' perspectives. Getting organized with a system that is user-friendly often takes some trial and error. Once you find one that works for you, you'll feel more secure about moving forward.

4 The Reflective Teacher, Metacognition, and the National Board Process

Six Word Memoir: Reflecting on teaching brings enlightening insight.
ANNIE, NM

Background

In the 1930s education philosopher and reformer, John Dewey wrote his explanation of *reflection* and its use in education. He wrote that reflection is a *skill different from and more rigorous than other forms of thought.* He described a specific mindset conducive to reflection: a reflective teacher is confident about his/her practice and abilities as a professional, but is willing to take action when evidence of needed change is identified and is able to consider new ideas, alternative actions and other points of view.

Metacognition, a term first used in 1979 by J. H. Flavell, is the skill of thinking about thinking. It concerns one's knowledge about one's own "knowing." It involves "noticing or identifying" something and then acting on that knowledge—in other words, analyzing and reflecting. Two particular kinds of teaching competencies contribute to analytic expertise: (1) subject or content knowledge and (2) pedagogical knowledge. Subject knowledge relates to content—the *what* of teaching. Pedagogical knowledge is the art and craft of teaching—the *how* of teaching.

Within these competencies are five distinct, yet interrelated skills:

- Setting goals.
- Teaching the lesson/content.
- Assessing whether goals are achieved.
- Analyzing why the goals were or were not achieved.
- Reflecting to revise the lesson.

Reflection is a special kind of self-analysis. In reflection, one looks back in order to look forward. One looks back, analyzes events or actions, then uses that analysis to make changes. In order to reflect and analyze the success of a lesson, and make decisions as to whether any revisions are needed, one must look back and analyze each step. The National Board has incorporated the competencies of subject knowledge and pedagogical knowledge, as well as the related skills of analyzing and reflecting into the National Board process.

- They are embedded in the Five Core Propositions and the Standards for each certificate.
- They mirror five of the six steps in the Architecture of Accomplished Teaching.
- They are the basis for many prompts in the Planning and Instruction, Analysis of Student Work, Analysis of the Video, and Reflection sections of the Written Commentary.

Most teachers are reflective by nature. But the National Board Certification process requires *reflection on steroids*. Never before will you have scrutinized your practice with such a fine-tooth comb. Never will you have looked at your students and your teaching decisions under a magnifying glass of such magnitude. The challenge is to get your thinking onto paper in a clear, consistent, and convincing way.

What Works!

Put your reflection skills to work on these questions about your lessons that are connected to the competencies and skills:

- What, specifically, were students to learn or be able to do during the lesson sequence?
- Why were the goals appropriate? How do you know?
- What strategies, activities, and learning environment factors did you use to teach the lesson?
- Why did you make those pedagogical decisions?
- What would evidence of learning look like?
- How do you know whether the learning did or did not take place?

- How did you assess the learning?
- Was the assessment directly tied to the learning goal? Did the assessment "match up" with the goal?
- What do your students do or say that provides evidence they did or did not learn the goal?
- What teacher actions led to learning (or not learning) the goal?
- What other factors influenced the learning?
- When you look back and analyze the goal setting, teaching, and assessment what evidence connects the learning to your teaching practice?
- How was your instruction a factor in the learning that did or did not take place?
- How might revisions in your lesson planning or implementation result in improvement?
- What revisions would you consider?
- How and why might those revisions result in a better outcome?

Why These Work!

Such questions are the essence of many of the prompts in Components 2, 3, and 4. Your ability to engage in metacognition to describe, analyze, and reflect on the competencies demonstrated in your teaching practice will determine the outcome of your efforts to become a National Board Certified Teacher (NBCT).

5 Writing for the National Board

Six-Word Memoir: Abandon beautiful wordage: Clear, consistent, convincing.
KRISTIN, AR

Present Your Case

Writing National Board entries is unlike any other kind of writing you've done. It's not like the creative writing assignments you did in high school or college. It's not even like writing a term paper or master's thesis. Your score isn't determined by your grammar or sentence structure, fancy language, or the number of research citations you include. In fact, some attributes of what is typically considered "good writing" don't necessarily apply here. So, what is it like?

Writing for the National Board is, above all else, *evidentiary*, meaning written to present *evidence*. Your sole purpose is to present evidence of your accomplished teaching, learning, leadership, and collaboration. It isn't quite as easy as pie, but it isn't rocket science either.

You must make a case for your accomplished teaching the same way a lawyer argues a case in the courtroom—by presenting strong *evidence*. You are the defendant acting as your own attorney, presenting evidence of what you do in your classroom. Your student work samples, videos, data, and responses to the prompts are the evidence of your accomplished teaching. The assessor is the judge and jury.

Overview of the Three Styles of Writing: Description, Analysis, and Reflection

Just as an attorney uses questioning styles to elicit evidence, the National Board uses writing styles that can be explained in three verbs: *describe*, *analyze*, and *reflect*. Each prompt connects to one or more writing styles to help you present information that is *clear, consistent,* and *convincing*. *Describe, analyze* and *reflect* are verbs that tell what you must *do*. The noun forms, *description, analysis* and *reflection*, are the *results* of your actions.

Description Tells What

When you describe something, you tell *about* it; you tell *what* occurred. In court, a witness gives the facts in order to paint a clear picture of a situation. There should be no interpretation or judgment in descriptive writing. In a National Board component, you respond with enough information for the assessor to form a picture or impression of what you want to depict. Key words in prompts that ask for description include:

| Tell | Explain | List | Describe | What |

A descriptive passage:

- Tells or retells the main facts.
- Is logically ordered.
- Has enough detail to set the scene and give assessors a basic sense of the class, student, or situation you need to describe.
- Contains accurate, precise enumeration wherever appropriate.
- Includes elements and features that allow an assessor to "see what you see."
- May be used in conjunction with analysis. You often need to describe the subject or situation you are analyzing so it is visible to the assessor, making the analysis more meaningful. However, the borders between them can be fuzzy.

Description in the Components

Description is the easiest type of writing to do. Most teachers find description easy to write and typically tend to describe way too much. Although it is effective to use description to give facts and paint a picture of your class, students, and activities, it isn't the most important type of writing. Why? *It is the least evidentiary of the writing styles.* Description sets the tone, draws a picture, and gives the facts. But it doesn't deliver much, if any, evidence. That is the task of analysis and reflection.

The *Instructional Context* section of Component 2, the *Writing About Planning* section of Component 3, and the various *Context Forms* of Components 3 and 4 are the largest descriptive passages you will write. These sections give assessors a sense of your teaching context and the featured class and student(s). Tell enough to give the assessors a realistic picture of the characteristics that shape your teaching and the personality of the class. Be sure to respond to every part of each prompt, but keep as close to page suggestion as possible (1 page in most certificates, two pages in some certificates) because you'll need space later for other, more evidence-rich sections of the components. Here are some *hypothetical* descriptive passages that might be found in a Component 2 Instructional Context:

- The featured class consists of twenty-seven students, who are eleven to fourteen years old. Science is the first period of the day. Several students are habitually tardy, which makes it difficult to begin instruction on time. Seven students are English Language Learners who leave ten minutes early to go to the Resource Room for language instruction. Therefore I must complete the essential lesson elements before they go. *EA/Science*
- Jenny is both young and immature for a fourth grader. She reads on a second grade level and has particular trouble putting her thoughts on paper. She often misspells words and writes entire stories without using any punctuation. She likes to work with a partner but has difficulty staying focused on the task. *MC/Generalist*
- All students in this AP Statistics class plan to attend a 4-year college. All students in the class have passed Algebra 2 and some are currently enrolled in Calculus 3. Nearly half of the students have taken an AP course, but none have taken any statistics courses prior to this class. *AYA/Math*
- The learners in this computer class vary in their linguistic and academic abilities and state reading scores. The majority of students are in the "Basic" reading category which is below grade level. Four students are "Below Basic" which signifies they are far below grade

level. Only one student in the whole class is "Proficient" and on grade level. The class personality is pleasant and cooperative, and most students are generally on-task. *EA/YA/Career and Technical Education*

Keep these points in mind when describing.

- Be succinct. Say enough to paint the picture then stop.
- Decide which facts and details are significant and emphasize those.
- Concentrate on facts and details that show an impact on teaching or learning.
- Resist the urge to tell *everything*. Details matter, but don't go on and on.
- Description should be the smallest portion of your writing.
- Follow suggested page limits. They are there for a reason—to keep you from writing too much description and not enough analysis and reflection.
- Support the description with details and examples—but not too many.

Analysis Asks So What and Why?

Description is the writing style that tells *what*. Analysis is the writing style that asks *so what?* and *why?* Compare it to an attorney who puts forth a theory, then goes about confirming or rejecting it depending on the evidence. Teachers make hundreds of decisions each day that are implicit in their knowledge of their students and content area, but seldom need to express this minutiae orally or in writing. However, the analysis questions in each component require this intrinsic knowledge be put into words on paper. Analytical writing is important because:

- It is the *most evidentiary* of the three styles.
- It demonstrates significance: *so what is it* and *why*?
- It shows the assessor the reasons and motives (rationale) for your actions and decisions.
- It interprets and justifies actions and decisions—backed up with evidence.

- It shows the assessor the thought processes you used to reach decisions.
- It examines why elements or events are described in certain ways.
- It involves taking apart what occurred during a teaching event.

Prompts that ask for analysis may contain these key words:

> How?   Why? In what ways . . .   Tell your rationale for . . .
> Explain why . . .

What Works! Using These Sentence Starters for Analytical Responses:

- I chose ___ because . . .
- There are several reasons why . . .
- The ___ on his paper showed me he didn't understand ___, so I . . .
- The rationale behind my decision to ___ was . . .
- This was significant because . . .
- This impacted student learning by . . .
- Because ___, therefore . . .
- In order to ___, I . . .

The subject(s) being analyzed (student work samples, assessment data, or a video) must be available for the assessors. Clearly label your samples and/or video and refer to them in the text. Assessors will look at the samples and videos to compare them to the evidence in your analysis. Typically, the assessor reads the forms first, then reads your component, and finally, looks at the work samples or video to see how tightly they support your writing and "match up". The analysis helps the assessors see the significance of the connections to evidence you submit.

Reflection Asks Now What?

The descriptive style of writing tells *what*—like a witness giving testimony or a journalist. The analytical style asks *so what* and *why*, like an attorney questioning a witness or a scientist. The reflective style goes a step further and asks *now what*? Reflection is like a jury looking back at the evidence to decide a case or a follow-up visit to a doctor to monitor a course of treatment. Reflection is a kind of self-analysis that:

- Explains the thought processes used *after* teaching a lesson/unit.
- Tells how you would make decisions in the future.
- Is retrospective.
- Explains the significance of a decision.
- Tells the impact of a decision, activity, or action.
- Reviews instructional strategy choices.
- Sets new goals based on your analytical conclusions.
- Demonstrates your understanding of the National Board Standards.

Prompts that require reflection ask you to look back at your teaching practice and/or to look ahead and predict what you might do differently. Analysis and reflection often go hand in hand and overlap. Reflective prompts may ask:

- What would you do differently if you were to teach the lesson again?
- What does the featured student's performance suggest about your teaching practice?
- Were these goals appropriate? Why?
- Were your lesson design, strategies, and materials appropriate? How do you know?
- How did students perform in light of the chosen goals?
- Could I have taken this a step further to increase student understanding?
- What have I experienced before that will help me make decisions now?
- What did I learn from this experience that will help me do even better next time?
- What did I learn about my teaching practice in relation to student learning?

Reflection assumes analysis has already taken place. A typical mistake teachers make is to retell, rather than reflect. When you reflect, you *explain* and *interpret* what happened, then tell what should come next. You look back then forward. A reflection is not a summary.

Use These Pointers for Reflection:

- Be honest. There is always something that can be done better. No lesson is perfect.
- Be realistic. Don't propose something that is clearly impossible.
- Focus on both the strengths and weaknesses of a lesson. No lesson is a total failure.
- Use concrete evidence to support your statements.
- Align and connect your instructional goals, the assessment activity, and your reflection on the lesson. There must be total consistency and agreement among them.
- Focus on the impact your teaching had on your students.

What Works! Using These Sentence Starters for Reflective Responses:

- In the future I . . .
- A key success was . . .
- An area for improvement is . . .
- My plan for the next lesson is . . .
- If I were to do this again . . .
- I learned ___ which will help me plan better next time by . . .
- Before this lesson, my students. . ., but because of this experience . . .
- Because of this teaching experience I learned. . .

Why These Work!

The boundaries between analysis and reflection are not clear-cut. Analysis focuses on *so what*, reflection focuses on *now what?* Analysis is about the past; reflection is about using the past to determine future actions. Understanding reflection will make your writing stronger.

Evidence or Lack of Evidence in Your Writing

Read and reflect on the following samples to see if you can tell the difference in the amount of evidence presented in each pair of examples:

- *#1. Lack of Evidence:* Rory had trouble writing complete responses to comprehension questions, so I gave him a graphic organizer to help him organize his thoughts and information. He was able to do better work.
- *#1. With Evidence:* To prepare the class for writing, I planned a reading comprehension activity. I directed students to read a text and answer questions about it. Rory was unable to write responses in complete sentences, and he also skipped questions. To determine Rory's reading level, I administered the DRA (Developmental Reading Assessment) and used informal assessments. I learned he could answer questions orally but struggled to put his thoughts on paper. Rory shared that when he saw a list of questions he felt overwhelmed. To address this problem, I began having him use a graphic organizer and assigned work in smaller chunks.
- *#2. Lack of Evidence:* My classroom is set up so kids can get their own supplies. One student from each group got supplies for their group. Each group set up their ramp and started rolling their cars down it to see how far they would travel. Marci's group rolled a car down their ramp, and it traveled a yard. They knew this because they measured with their string and a yardstick.
- *#2. With Evidence:* I set up my science lab and centers to encourage easy access to all materials and to give adequate space for the inquiry activity. In the beginning of the video, Marci was easily able to retrieve from the supply bins the string and yardstick her group needed to measure the distance their car rolled off the ramp. She and her group also had space to place their ramp and have room for the car to roll. When the car came to a stop after rolling down the ramp, they used the string to measure from the bottom of the ramp to the front end of the car. They laid the string on a yardstick to measure the distance in inches and feet. Sam measured first and declared the distance to be 3 feet. Lynn said, "That is a yard. Our car traveled a yard!" I asked the others in the group if they agreed. Marci replied, "Yes, 3 feet is the

same as a yard." This showed me everyone in that group understood the measuring equivalents.

- *#3: Lack of Evidence:* I used materials and realia from Mexico, Costa Rica, Spain, and Panama for this lesson to provide a more concrete visual of the foreign country. The kids really liked using these "real" materials.
- *#3: With Evidence:* I used a variety of authentic materials and realia for this lesson to provide a more concrete visual of the foreign country. I used a map of Mexico, pictures from a Costa Rican calendar, newspapers from Spain, posters from a travel company, photographs from books, and magazine ads promoting Panama as a tour destination.

What Works!

Give specific examples in your Written Commentary to give a clear, consistent and convincing picture of your accomplished teaching. *EXAMPLES = EVIDENCE.*

Why These Work!

Specific examples build a strong wall of evidence!

DANGER: Style Mistakes and Pitfalls

While learning to write with the three styles of writing, some writing hazards emerge. Watch out for these and avoid them:

- *Missing Person Alert* Q: What is missing from this hypothetical passage?
  The students were introduced to their new vocabulary by using flash cards. After practicing as a whole group, they were divided into study groups. First, they were assigned jobs within the group. Each group was provided with a set of flashcards and a worksheet to reinforce their learning.

Q: *What is wrong with the above passage?* A: *The teacher is missing*! Nowhere in that passage is the teacher mentioned. Who is the teacher? Where is the teacher? When writing your entries, don't hide in the background, be invisible. You must put yourself in the picture—clearly, consistently and convincingly. How do you do that?

A: *How to fix it:* I introduced students to their new vocabulary using flash cards. After practicing as a whole group, I divided them into study groups. First I assigned jobs within the group then I provided a set of flashcards and worksheet to reinforce their learning. Note also, that passive voice verbs (were introduced, was provided) are replaced with active voice verbs.

What Works! Making Yourself Visible Within Your Writing

- Write in the first person. Use the pronoun I frequently. Candidates often feel writing about themselves is bragging and that feels uncomfortable. Put those feelings aside and
- Use first-person pronouns in order to showcase your actions.
- Be careful with the pronoun *we*. It takes more space, but it is stronger to say, the students and I, rather than *we*. That way it's clear just who *we* is. YOU are in the picture. Use *we* sparingly. Use it once, then switch back to *I*.
- In Component 4, when using *we* to show collaboration, use it once or twice, then turn the focus to your own contribution and switch to *I* or *my*: I collaborated with my department to plan the science fair. *We* each had assigned roles. *My* role was to. . .
- Use the active voice because it is clearer, more direct, and more concise. Go back and look at the example passage. Not only is the teacher missing, the verbs are almost all written in the passive voice. Sentences using passive voice verbs are wordier, longer, and less clear than those using the active voice. The "fixed" example uses active voice verbs.
- Use *helping verbs, by,* and *-ing* endings sparingly. For example, say: *I provided flashcards . . .* instead of *Flashcards were provided,* or, *I was providing . . .* After writing a draft, go back and highlight each verb

phrase with a helper and/or -ing. Then rewrite as many as possible in the active voice.

Look again at the rewritten passage with pronouns that put the teacher into the picture and with active voice verbs. Do you now see the differences?

Why This Works!

This passage is much stronger because the teacher is clearly in the picture, and the active voice verbs show who performed the actions expressed. There are also details to demonstrate how this teacher's actions support the National Board Standards. This lets the assessor know who led the lesson and how the teacher produced learning.

More Writing Mistakes and Pitfalls:

- *Preaching from the Pulpit:* This occurs when the candidate uses the Written Commentary as a soapbox. Avoid inserting personal views and frustrations about teaching into the Written Commentary. It is a waste of words and space. In a nutshell, accomplished teachers are able to demonstrate accomplished teaching and student learning in spite of difficulties and obstacles. Assessors score only *evidence* of accomplished teaching, so it is important to use words and space to demonstrate your evidence.
- *The E.S.P. Communicator:* When candidates don't explain their actions and decisions clearly, the assessor is left to connect the dots. Be careful not to assume your reasons for choices are so obvious no explanation is needed. Some candidates may be clear about what they *do*, but may write ambiguously or not at all about the thinking processes that led them to a particular decision. This is a common pitfall, especially among more experienced candidates whose actions have become so intuitive and automatic they no longer deliberately think about the reasons for their decisions.
- It may seem tedious or annoying to be pressed into the deeper thinking the analysis and reflection sections require. But you must explain the thinking and decision making processes behind your decisions that you applied to student work samples, videos or other

artifacts used in the components. Never assume an assessor will "see" evidence without an explanation. Explain your decisions and choices clearly.

- *The Feelings Guru:* This candidate substitutes feelings for concrete evidence. Work to eliminate all *I believe, I feel, I tried*, and *I think* statements from your writing. Although teachers are very caring people, the National Board components are not the place to lay out your personal teaching philosophy or beliefs. Statements such as *I believe all children can learn . . .* or, *I feel all students should . . .* , however true, are irrelevant to the process. The assessor looks for *evidence* of a teacher's effectiveness, but a teacher's philosophy is not a measurable piece of evidence. Assessors look for evidence in the form of specific examples, descriptions, analysis, reflection, and artifacts such as student work samples, assessment data, and videos. Avoid these pitfalls by returning to the trial lawyer analogy. You must present evidence clearly, convincingly, and consistently to the assessors who are the judge and jury.

- *Jargon:* This is the specialized language, words, and terms used within a profession. Use it sparingly. Too much educational jargon gets in the way of understanding. The best writing is plain, simple, easily understood language—the kind you use when you talk. This especially applied to acronyms. Use them sparingly and always spell them out completely the first time used.

What Works! Using Strong Verbs, Strong Phrases, and Bloom's Taxonomy

Writing strong National Board entries does not require a fancy vocabulary. The assessors come from all fifty states, big cities, and small towns, and are teachers just like you. Ask yourself whether anyone, from anywhere, will understand what you wrote and you'll be on the right track.

Strong verbs and Phrases describe accomplished teaching actions and qualities that have meaning within the National Board Certification process. They are words that help you showcase your teaching practice as described in the Standards. They are, for the most part, plain, strong verbs and descriptive phrases. Using these verbs and phrases in your writing can lend clarity and strength to your descriptions, analyses, and reflections. But the criteria for using them are authenticity and honesty. They must have meaning within the context of your teaching practice. Here are some examples:

- *Strong Verbs:* I encouraged, developed, designed, guided, supported, organized, facilitated, chose, chose to, selected, challenged, provided, gave, taught, engaged, demonstrated, learned, modeled, measured, asked, practiced, assigned, performed, contributed, impacted, influenced, instructed, questioned.

- *Strong Phrases:* students as risk-takers; ways of learning; learning community; lifelong learner; build self esteem; promote student understanding; appropriate assessment; constructive feedback; fairness; equity; goal related; integrated learning; behavior intervention; active engagement/listening; high expectations; insightful questions; meaningful; learning goals; outcome based; reluctant learner; on task; rich and in-depth; inclusion; productive classroom; cooperative groups; parent partnerships.

- *More Strong Phrases:* community involvement; collaboration; and diverse perspectives; beyond the classroom; high expectations; problem solving; real-world applications; rich variety of sources; student ownership; teacher as a learner; teaching strategies; unique learning needs; varied assessments; work collaboratively; standards-based; content-oriented; application; direct impact on student learning; I learned; I should have; now I understand; relevant characteristics; and motivational.

- *Bloom's Taxonomy* is one of the best references for finding effective verbs that indicate levels of learning and for planning appropriate lessons. Here is a recap (the lowest to highest levels):

    Remembering: define, memorize, record, identify, label, list, locate, match, name, recall, spell, tell, state, underline, recognize, repeat

    Understanding: restate, discuss, describe, explain, express, identify, interpret, paraphrase, put in order, restate, retell, summarize, review

    Applying: apply, conclude, construct, use, dramatize, illustrate, show, sketch, draw, give a new example, solve, operate, practice, translate

Analyzing: distinguish, analyze, differentiate, appraise, experiment, compare, contrast, diagram, debate, categorize, classify, dissect, infer

Evaluating: defend, judge, value, evaluate, support, argue, appraise.

Creating: assemble, construct, create, design, develop, formulate, write

Why These Work!

These verbs provide evidence in your writing. They indicate your deliberate participation in the processes that make up accomplished teaching and are examples of the "language" used in the Standards that show evidence of accomplished teaching.

Apply the litmus test to decide if something meets the criteria for being universally understood. There must be no confusion about the terms used in the Written Commentary. This is especially true for the names of programs or materials you or your school utilizes. Be sure to spell them out and give a brief explanation. Examples:

- STEAM (Science, Technology, Engineering, Arts, Mathematics) Education . . .
- NCTM, the National Council of Teachers of Mathematics

What Works! Creating a Writing Framework

- Make the case you are an accomplished teacher by showing evidence of exemplary teaching. You are the lawyer. The assessors are the judge and jury.
- Connect the three styles of writing to the prompts: description, analysis, and reflection.
- Keep description to a minimum. Description tells *what*.
- Analysis asks *so what* and *why* and is the most evidentiary type of writing.
- Reflection asks *now what* and is a type of self-analysis.
- Provide concrete examples of your actions and decisions.

- Write in the first person as much as possible.
- Use strong verbs and the active voice.
- Avoid using large amounts of educational jargon.
- Use buzz verbs, buzz phrases, and Bloom's Taxonomy language where appropriate.
- Be authentic.

Why These Work!

Your writing is the "legal brief" of your portfolio. It contains all the evidence to show the assessors you are an accomplished teacher.

What Works! Following the 3Cs in the Level 4 Rubric:

Clear: Never assume anything and explain everything

Consistent: Goals, activities, assessments, etc., must match up and be connected

Convincing: Build a wall of evidence with examples

Add more Cs:

Concise: Make your point and move on. Write short, to-the point sentences.

Correct: Use correct grammar and punctuation so the assessor can focus on your content.

Concrete: Evidence needs to be specific, real, and measurable, not vague and ambiguous.

Style Tips:

- Limit bolding, underlining, and CAPS. A little goes a long way.
- Be as consistent as possible with verb tenses.

- Talk to the assessor, not at the assessor. The assessor is your audience.
- Write in your own voice. Don't lose yourself in the writing process.
- State the *significance* of events.
- Avoid acronyms unless you are sure the assessor will understand them or can explain them.
- Streamline writing and cut the fluff. Edit! Edit! Edit numerous times!
- Avoid *helping verbs* and *-ing* forms of verbs wherever possible.

Be Sure To:

- Back up your writing on your computer often!
- Pay attention to page limits. The assessors stop reading when they reach the limit.
- Follow portfolio instructions exactly.
- Answer *all* parts of every question/prompt. Respond *to* the question, not *about* it.
- Show the impact on student learning.
- Connect your teaching practice to the standards.
- Study the Architecture of Accomplished Teaching for insight into the prompts.
- Give up stressing about the vagueness of the prompts. It will only drive you crazy.

Why These Work! Clear, consistent, convincing writing showcases your evidence.

6 Probing the Prompts

Six Word Memoir: I thought I already answered that!
TANIKA, MS

The Structure of The Prompts

Understanding the language and intent of the prompts can be a challenge. Candidates often feel they are answering the same thing multiple times, and the language often can be difficult to decipher. "If only I understood what they are asking!" is a candidate's lament. Each prompt is written to help you provide evidence of the Standards in your teaching practice and here is a revelation—they generally follow the steps in the Architecture of Accomplished Teaching!

Notice the directions for each section ask you to *address or respond to* the questions, *not answer* them. This is more than just a nuance of language; there is a very important distinction between the two terms. *Address and respond* mean to write what is true for you in your teaching context. *Answer* implies something more "black or white," right or wrong. The prompts allow for open-ended responses that fit your teaching context. So there isn't just one way to demonstrate accomplished teaching. The prompts don't dictate any particular teaching style.

Component 2 is "rich" in writing, so going into depth to discuss how to probe the prompts is important. Many of the strategies discussed can be used in Components 3 and 4 as well.

Component 2: Differentiation in Instruction

The *Instructional Context/Student Profile* (ENS certificate) in every certificate area sets the tone for the Written Commentary. You might compare it to the ambiance of a restaurant which sets the scene for your dining experience. The writing style for this section is largely descriptive—you are painting the picture of your classroom context. Yours may ask for information about a *class*, a *subgroup* such as students with exceptional needs, or about an *individual* and the prompts may differ from certificate to certificate. Read *your* Instructional Context/Student Profile carefully.

Take the Prompts Apart: MCGen Example of an Instructional Context

Sometimes it helps to break a prompt apart and make a list of what it asks for. Since the prompts in the Instructional Context are the same or nearly the same for many certificates across Component 2, the MCGen prompts might serve as an example for many certificate areas.

Prompt 1: School Setting:

- My school (pre-school, elementary, middle/high, charter, rural, urban, suburban)
- Subject of the component
- Number of students in the class you are using for this component.
- Ages of students in the class (must be within the age range allowed in your certificate).
- Grade(s) of students in this class.

Prompt 2: Relevant characteristics of the class that influence your instructional strategies for this theme or topic of concern? Think: What is meant by *relevant*? Synonyms include *pertinent, applicable, significant, and important.*

- Ethnic diversity
- Cultural diversity
- Linguistic diversity (students and/or parents)
- Range of abilities (reading/math levels, gifted/talented, receives remedial services, etc.)
- Personality of the class (competitive, cooperative, etc.)

Prompt 3: Relevant characteristics of students with exceptional needs and abilities that influenced your planning for this theme or topic of concern?

- Range of abilities: the lowest to highest.
- Cognitive challenges: Gifted students may be considered to have exceptional needs.

- Social/behavioral challenges
- Attention issues
- Sensory issues
- Physical challenges

Prompt 4: The relevant features of your teaching context that influenced your selection of this theme or topic.

- Available resources (or lack of resources)
- Scheduling (pull-out periods, special classes, etc.)
- Room allocation (shared space, in a pod, in a portable structure away from the building)

Prompt 5: Particular instructional challenges do the students chosen represent for this lesson sequence.

- Students' skills and abilities
- Previous experiences and learning related to the topic
- Class dynamics

The relevant characteristics described in the Instructional Context/Student Profile should appear again in the Written Commentary. It's not enough just to *tell* the relevant characteristics. In the Written Commentary, you must show yourself *using your knowledge* of the characteristics you wrote about. You must connect them with evidence. If you can't, the characteristic may not be relevant enough to include at all.

Reminder: Prompt examples above may not exactly fit all certificate areas and are used only to model how to take the prompts apart to focus on key words. Use only YOUR certificate prompts.

Aligning the Instructional Context/Student Profile Responses in Components

You may not be able to write one Instructional Context/Student Profile and cut and paste it intact for other components/forms that ask for an Instructional Context. The *slant or lens* of the Instructional Context varies for each component because each needs to focus on a different class and/or subject area. The relevant characteristics of a science or social studies class might differ greatly from those of a writing group. Teachers who are departmentalized know that the personality and relevant characteristics of each period's class differ. The first class of the day can be very different from the last class of the day. Even within the same group of students in a self-contained classroom, the instructional challenges and class dynamics can vary from subject to subject, and even time of day. So each component's Instructional Context section, whether in the Written Commentary or on a Form/Sheet, must focus on the characteristics of each particular class, student, or subject area.

For example, in the MCGen Component 2 Instructional Context, a relevant characteristic might be that several students have difficulty with the editing step of the writing process. But for the Component 3 Video Instructional Context Sheet, that information might not be relevant because the video doesn't focus on writing. For Component 3, to give background and fit the topics of the videos, one might write that students arrived in fourth grade with little previous science instruction or that several students are in a pull-out math resource program. So keep in mind that information from the Component 2 Instructional Context/Student Profile can't always be cut and pasted identically into other components.

Information in the Instructional Context/Student Profile needs to be connected to information in the Written Commentary. For example, if you state you provide a slant board, special writing paper, or a software program to aid with writing, assessors would expect to find these accommodations referenced later in the Written Commentary.

Component 2: The Planning and Instruction Section

If the Instructional Context/Student Profile is the ambiance of the component, the Planning and Instruction section is the appetizer. Again, this section may have different names in different certificates. Here you:

- Present your plans, overall goals, and objectives for the lesson sequence.
- Explain the rationale for the choices you made.
- Show how the learning was meaningful.

A key understanding about the prompts in all sections of the Written Commentary is that they are connected to the Architecture of Accomplished Teaching (AAT). That means they are also connected to the Core Propositions and the Standards. So prompts in the Planning and Instruction generally follow Steps 1–4 of the AAT. This isn't written in stone, but it's a pattern generally evident in Components 2 and 3. Steps 5 and 6 are embedded in the Reflection Sections. For example, Prompt #5 in the Planning and Teaching Analysis Section of the MCGen Component 2 is: *What were your specific objectives for the writing assignments for the class in general and these students in particular? Explain why you identified these objectives and how they are appropriate for the students in your class.* This prompt would largely fall on Step 2 of the AAT: *Set high and worthwhile goals.*

Analysis Section

The Instructional Context/Student Profile sets the tone, like the ambiance in a restaurant. The Planning and Instruction was the appetizer. The Analysis of Students' Responses in Component 2 or the Written Commentary prompts in Component 3 are like the entrée, or main course. The prompts in these sections require both specific examples and references to the student work samples and/or the videos.

Analyzing the Prompts

Every certificate has this prompt in Component 3:

How did you establish a fair, equitable, and challenging environment for all students? Cite specific examples from the video recording.

Break the prompt into its parts:

- *Fair*: The assignment was appropriate for learning level; appropriate expectations.
- *Equitable*: The lesson is designed to address what each student needs to succeed; choice built into lesson to address learning styles; varied time allocation to complete work. Opportunities exits to participate and learn; materials available and easily in reach; student can reach all resources from his wheelchair independently.

- *Challenging:* Objectives are within reach of students' abilities, but may require the acquisition of new skills/learning to accomplish.
- Refer to your certificate Standard for additional examples.

Fabricated EA/Science Video Written Commentary Example: "When the video begins, students are finishing their construction of a variety of ramps based on previous learning about Newton's Laws of Motion *(fair)*. I formed groups to accommodate learning styles and personalities, and each group decided on the roles each member would have *(equitable)*. I gave each group choices in the materials to cover the surface of their ramp *(equitable)*. Group 3's materials and the ramp are on a table instead of the floor so that Tina, in a wheelchair, can easily participate. I provided a picture card illustrating the directions for Aiden, who is autistic, and his aide is available for help as needed *(fair, equitable)*. Students had choices within the activity to make the activity more or less challenging based on their previous knowledge and understanding of Newton's Laws of Motion *(challenging environment).*"

What Works!

Digging deep into your students' work or the video.

- Answer *all* parts of every prompt. Respond *to* the prompt, not *about* it.
- Scrutinize the work samples/video to identify the students' strengths and difficulties.
- Write about specific strategies that resulted in learning and fostered the students' academic development.
- Tell how the information helped you move them forward intellectually.
- Tell how you promoted the students' personal responsibility for learning.

Why This Works!

The Analysis section showcases your knowledge of teaching and learning by explaining your thinking that you know what actions you took and what decisions you made to show accomplished teaching.

Didn't I Just Answer That?

Candidates are often frustrated because it sometimes seems the questions are redundant, and it can feel as if you are answering the same question again. But that isn't really the case. Following are two prompts found in the Analysis of Student Work section of the *AYA/English Language Arts* Component 2 that sound much alike:

- *The Student as a Reader: What about the student as an individual provides insight into his/her work samples and your analysis of them?*
- *The Student as a Writer: What about the student as an individual provides insight into his/her writing samples and your analysis of them?*

Now consider these prompts from the *EMC/Literacy* Component 2:

- Description and Analysis of Student Work Sample #1:
  What feedback did you provide to the student regarding his or her writing and ability to construct meaning through writing in this assignment?
- Description and Analysis of Student Work Sample #2:
  What feedback did you provide to the student? How did this feedback help the student continue to grow as a writer and to construct meaning through writing?

Reading these sets of prompts, they appear very similar. However, each contains a term and/or nuance that means the response to each prompt must be different. In the ELA prompts, the candidate must discern differences in student performances in *reading* and then in *writing*. There could be some overlap, but clear differences will also likely be discussed. In the Literacy example, both ask about feedback but refer to *different assignments*. So the lens on uses to view the assignments would be different. The responses must be specific to the questions asked.

What Works!

Analyze what is alike and what is different in prompts that sound alike. You may need to respond using a different perspective or lens.

Reflection Section

In this chapter, you've experienced the ambiance (Instructional Context/Student Profile), sampled the appetizer (Planning and Instruction), and savored the main course (Analysis of Student Work). Last is the dessert or aperitif: *Reflection*. It may have the fewest prompts, but what it lacks in numbers, it makes up for in the depth of thinking that thoughtful responses require. Reflection is actually a particular kind of analysis—self-analysis. Self-analysis is what the reflection prompts ask you to do. You have to look inward and backward for these responses, which, like all responses in the components, show evidence of the Propositions and Standards.

Here are two reflection questions from the *AYA/History-Social Studies*, Component 2:

- *1) How successful was your use of differentiation in instruction in meeting the academic needs of the featured students?*

Again, break the prompt into parts and respond to each separately:

- How successful? One hundred percent? Somewhat? Mostly?
- Differentiation examples
- Evidence? Observation? Test scores? Completed assignment? Discussion?

Be honest with this appraisal. Cite specific examples.

- *2) If you were given the opportunity to use these assignments/prompts again, what, if anything, would you do differently? Explain your answer.*
- Look back to analyze the success of the lesson, then look ahead and tell what you could do differently that would address areas you wish had been better.
- No lesson is perfect, so there are ALWAYS areas that could be better. The assessors expect you to want the next lesson to be even better.

What Works! Writing a Thoughtful Reflection

- Be honest. The assessors are teachers like you. They work with kids every day too. Although the evidence in the Written Commentary will give them a good indication of the impact of the lesson sequence on the students' learning, let them know you are aware of areas that could be improved. You tried your best, but if everything didn't work out quite the way you planned just say so. Recognizing where improvement could happen provides evidence!

- Write a meaningful reflection. Refrain from saying everything about the lesson went perfectly and you wouldn't change a thing. Most lessons are more like country songs—filled with ups and downs. There is always something that can be done better.
- Write a balanced reflection. Reflection isn't only about what went wrong or what you would change; talk about the positives too. Reflection should show you think about all aspects of your lessons and their impact on student learning.

Why These Work!

There is no perfect lesson. Each has its own strengths and weaknesses. Showing you recognize them shows your depth of knowledge of your subject matter and pedagogy, and your ability to reflect on your practice.

What Works!

Use the examples in the *Template for Responding to Prompts* in the Appendix to see how to respond to nearly all types of prompts. The figure contains examples from several certificate areas and all four components. It shows how to use your notes/evidence and the prompts themselves to construct responses that are clear, consistent, and convincing.

Component 2
Differentiation and Writing About Student Work

Six Word Memoir: Work samples reveal my teaching's impact.
DOUG, CA

Component 2: Focusing on Student Work

Component 2 in all certificates centers on differentiation of instruction and the analysis of student work samples. In the Music certificate, the Component 2 takes the form of a video because of the performance nature of music. Other certificates ask for more typical samples. Many certificates ask for writing samples. Some certificates ask for student work samples generated from activities and/or projects. For this component, you collect student work samples from a series of lessons, then *describe, analyze, and reflect* on the work of one or more students using examples that show growth over time. The work samples are the evidence of student learning, the effectiveness of your planning and teaching, your implementation of the Architecture of Accomplished Teaching, and your ability to describe, analyze, and reflect on your teaching practice.

School districts currently require teachers to document student achievement primarily through standardized test scores. The NBPTS cares about student achievement but recognizes a variety of ways in addition to test scores that learning can be demonstrated. Here, your analysis of student work is important because it is the means by which you evaluate your students' learning and the effectiveness of your teaching. When grading, teachers look for evidence in student work that shows understanding of the content. But in the National Board process, the assessors go deeper. They look at your *analysis* of student work to see what *evidence/examples of effective teaching* it provides.

The measure of accomplished teaching is its capacity to impact student learning. Effective teaching means that, as a result of your teaching practice, student learning improves. That is why you need to plan the lesson sequence and choose the students and work you feature in this component carefully. That said, it does sometimes happen that students don't show the growth hoped for. The key thought, if that happens, is being able to analyze the cause for the lack of growth and make new plans. Effective teaching relies on the teacher's knowledge of students and subject matter and the ability to plan engaging, appropriate lessons for *these students, at this time, in this setting,* whether growth occurs or not.

What Works! Planning the Lesson Sequence with the End in Mind

Teaching a lesson, then crossing your fingers and hoping the evidence the assessors expect to see is there, is not the smartest plan. Your goal is to satisfy the Level 4 Scoring Rubric and *planning backwards* is an effective strategy to use. By that I mean design your lesson sequence to fit the component instructions and Written Commentary prompts, rather than trying to make the requirements fit your lessons. Like planning a trip, you must have the destination in mind in order to get there. Plan lessons that embed the evidence assessors expect to see into the lesson. This is not cheating; it is smart planning!

Planning a Lesson Backwards

- Start with the evidence assessors expect to see. The Level 4 Rubric in your Instructions and Scoring Guide lays out the expectations.
- The 3Cs of *clear, consistent, and convincing* in the rubric should become your mantra.
- Read the bulleted list on your Level 4 Rubric. These items are the evidence you need in the lessons to demonstrate in your teaching practice.
- Include each bulleted piece of evidence in your lessons and show in the Written Commentary how it is connected to your teaching and the student work.

- Planning backwards will assure you've addressed the steps on the Architecture of Accomplished Teaching.

The way to show *clear, consistent, and convincing* evidence to the assessors is to use the student work samples to explain exactly what you did and why. The assessors have only your written work and samples to look at. They are your only avenues of communication with the assessors.

What Works! Planning a Lesson Using the Level 4 Rubric

What might it look like to incorporate the Level 4 Rubric evidence into the planning of your lessons? To illustrate a teacher's thinking process, using the Middle Childhood Generalist (MC Gen) Rubric as an example, read the *hypothetical* notes a teacher might write when planning the student work component to include the evidence from the Rubric.

RUBRIC: The Level 4 performance provides clear, consistent, and convincing evidence that the teacher recognizes students' individual learning differences and past experiences to set high, worthwhile, and appropriate goals for student learning and connects instruction to those goals. Teacher's Thinking:

- I'll pre-assess/take a writing sample to determine where my students are in the writing process, then plan specific activities to address those needs.
- I'll plan differentiated writing experiences over a period of time that address the learning differences represented in my class.
- I'll plan narrative and expository prompts that my students will find interesting.
- I'll provide reference and vocabulary materials for my new English speakers.

Why These Work!

You can see how much information about the teaching process is embedded in the thinking notes and how it references the Architecture of Accomplished

Teaching and the Component 2, Level 4 Rubric. The Written Commentary needs to reveal the thinking that went into the planning of the lessons and the actions you took to put the ideas into practice. That provides strong evidence of the rubric.

One last point: did you notice how each statement began with *I*? And other first-person references such as *my* were used? Count them. First person is the strongest voice to use when explaining your teaching practice. Strong voice adds value to your writing.

What Works! Choosing Students to Feature

In all certificate areas, whether on paper or video:

- Choose students for whom there is something to say. Select students for whom your teaching has *clearly, consistently, and convincingly* made a difference.
- Select students through whom you can *clearly, consistently, and convincingly* show the range of your teaching abilities.
- Select students whose work allows you to *clearly, consistently, and convincingly* demonstrate the effectiveness of your teaching strategies through differentiation.

Why These Works!

Selecting students for whom there is something to say allows you to showcase your knowledge of students, content, and pedagogy.

What Works! Choosing Work Samples to Feature

- Choose samples that demonstrate the effectiveness of your teaching strategies.
- Choose tasks worthy of your students' time and effort.
- Choose samples that support the goals and objectives of the lessons.

- Choose complex assignments that challenge students' thinking and show their learning across disciplines—toss most worksheets and multiple choice assessments.
- Choose assignments that feature open-ended questions or prompts. They are strong choices because they provide an avenue for creativity, critical thinking, and showing understanding. Most worksheets don't do that.
- Choose samples that allow students to demonstrate a range of understanding of the content.
- Choose samples that show progression of learning and progress over time.
- Choose samples with meaningful feedback from you. Go beyond *good job* or grammar and spelling corrections. The feedback should show specific guidance that will help the student know how to improve next time. Example: *You used commas correctly in this writing!* OR *Remember to use commas with words in a series.*

Why These Work!

Choosing work samples carefully allows you to showcase your strategies, accomplished teaching, and student growth.

What Works! Save Examples of the Following:

- Evaluation rubrics—yours and student-made ones provide strong evidence of self-assessment and student engagement.
- Sets of work or copies (color copies if possible) from several students. Some teachers keep class sets. This will give you the widest selection. Date all work.
- A variety of types of work that pertain to your lesson sequence.
- Save more than you think you will need in case a student moves away.
- Take photos of work samples such as projects or 3-D samples.
- Make sure work samples and instructional materials follow the directions for the type of work the component requires, for all specifications, and address the goals of the lessons.

Why This Works!

These types of examples give you choices, showcase your thinking and your strategies, and give evidence of your explicit instruction.

Analyzing Student Work

Planning and teaching the lessons that produce the student work samples show evidence of four of the Five Core Propositions and the Standards. They show:

- Evidence of your knowledge of your students (Proposition 1)
- Evidence of knowledge of your content area (Proposition 2)
- Evidence that you think systematically about your practice (Proposition 3)
- Evidence that you manage and monitor your students' learning (Proposition 4)

Analyzing student work to the depth required for Component 2 is very different from typical day-to-day grading. Grading papers usually entails assigning a mark, score, or symbol such as smiley face, star, or percentage, returning the paper, and going on to the next topic. But grading papers that way, isn't really analysis. Think of analysis as *insight*—what you *see in* a student's work, what the work *tells* you about student learning. Analyzing means looking at student work in order to understand and improve it.

- Notice *how* students demonstrate their understanding of the learning goal.
- Notice *which skills* the student already knows.
- Notice *misconceptions* about the learning goal.
- Notice the *mistakes* the student makes.
- Notice *indicators* that the activity was successful or unsuccessful.
- Decide *what the student needs next* to achieve the learning goal. This is part of the *differentiation* element of Component 2.

What Works! Your Analysis of Work Samples Shows Accomplished Teaching.

- Be *specific* when analyzing and writing about student work.
- Add *details* to your writing to show your understanding of a student's learning—or lack of learning. This is how assessors evaluate your level of knowledge. For example, saying that a student *can't subtract* really doesn't say much at all. Instead, show that you know *why* the student can't subtract. Example: *A student makes subtraction errors because:*
    - The student subtracts inaccurately over zeros.
    - The student has trouble borrowing from numbers larger than three digits.
    - The student makes errors because columns aren't aligned.
    - The student doesn't know the subtraction facts.

After you analyze for specificity, plan your instruction to include what the student needs next (flashcard drill, graph paper to align columns, hands-on materials, etc.) to address the deficit. This demonstrates your knowledge of subject, how to teach it, and your NB Standards. Such actions demonstrate your ability to *differentiate* according to student need.

Why This Works!

The kind of analysis teachers do every day connects to strong evidence of what accomplished teachers should know and be able to do and makes your thinking visible. *Analysis leads to differentiation.*

Looking for Evidence in Student Work

Why does the National Board have a component based on student work? Through student work samples, the assessor can see how you address the steps on the *Architecture of Accomplished Teaching*—how you do the following:

- Set appropriate, high, worthwhile goals.
- Choose appropriate, engaging materials and activities that will move students toward achieving the goals. Differentiate according to student need.
- Plan and deliver effective instruction.
- Adjust goals and instruction based on student performance.
- Use analysis of student work to assess and plan the next learning steps, and set new goals.

Now imagine that you've planned and taught lessons about an important topic for your component. You collected stacks of student work samples that support the goals and objectives and represent the activities and assessments you planned. You've chosen the student(s) for whom there is something to say, and their work samples and your notes are beside you at the computer. You are ready to tackle the prompts in Component 2. You are ready to start writing. But where and how do you start?

What Evidence Shows

Start by locating the evidence in the body of work you've collected. Evidence is an *example* that supports something you assert to be true. Choose evidence along a continuum from weak to strong that is most convincing. Specific examples are evidence that show:

- Students engaged with the lesson's goal(s).
- How the materials and activities you use help the student(s) meet the learning goal.
- How you manage and monitor their learning.
- How you modify and adjust instruction to meet students' needs.
- How do you assess student work in relation to the stated goal(s).
- How you use the analysis of student work to plan the next steps.

Note! These represent steps in the Architecture of Accomplished Teaching.

Writing about Evidence in Student Work

Respond to each prompt with information that is true for the featured student(s). Discuss your analysis of their work and *cite specific examples* that have led you to these conclusions. Break the prompts into parts, paying particular attention to the verbs such as *describe, cite, or explain*, that will clarify what *you do* or the *student does* and what you write about. Pay attention to the nouns you are asked to address. These might include *behaviors, evidence, or patterns*.

Consider this fabricated example from the AYA/ELA certificate and look for specific evidence: *To help Student A expand her reading repertoire, I provided a variety of texts including art magazines, dramatic presentations, cartoons, movies, TV shows, novels, Twitter feeds, and editorials, which resulted in her identifying that reading can take multiple forms and that she can find texts that suit and expand her outside interests. She used to think that reading was a chore and read only what was required for school. But now she often shares in her journal what she's reading about and comments on what she learns from the reading and how it provides an escape from her personal struggles.* What evidence is shown in this passage? The teacher:

- References the goal (expand Student A's reading repertoire).
- Gives specific examples of materials/strategies used to address the goal.
- Explains the teacher's actions (role) and the result (Student A can now find texts that interest her).
- Explains how the student has changed/grown in relation to the goal.

What Works!

Give specific examples in your writing.

Why This Works! Each example is evidence that supports the effectiveness of your teaching.

Writing to Make Thinking Visible About Student Work

Not explaining their thinking and/or decisions may be the most common error candidates make when writing about student work. It's easy to point out what the student(s) did or didn't do in a work sample, but too often candidates don't write about their own role within the learning sequence. Sometimes this is because the teacher's actions have become so automatic that the candidate almost doesn't consciously pay attention to them anymore. Other times the candidate simply fails to mention the choices and decisions made because he/she thinks the assessor will just "know" or assume. This is a grave mistake in the National Board process. Although candidates write about student growth, what the National Board assessor is really looking for is evidence about the candidate's *teaching practice*. Don't let a blind spot undermine your writing when it comes to instructional decisions and choices *you make!*

What Works!

- Write in the first person. Use *I* statements frequently.
- Use sentence starters/stems such as:

I chose ___ because ___.
Because I know Tim ___, I ___.
I differentiated for Laura when I ___.
When I saw ___, I realized ___.
The reasons I chose ___ were ___.
I saw the error was caused by ___ so I ___.
As a result of ___, Jennifer was able to ___.
I used a variety of strategies including ___, ___, and ___.

Why This Works! Explaining your actions makes your thinking visible. Using sentence stems that show *cause and effect* as evidence shows strong analysis. The student work component is really about examining your teaching practice through the lens of student work samples and differentiation. Student work samples are the vehicle through which you differentiate, analyze, and reflect.

Analyzing student work is among the most important things teachers do because it has such a significant impact on student learning. You are already experienced with this skill! But you may not have had to analyze and reflect on it in written form until now. Writing clearly, consistently, and convincingly showcases your accomplished teaching. This component is an opportunity to let your expertise shine through.

8 Writing for Component 3
The Video Component

Six Word Memoir: Do I really look and sound like that?
PAULA, PA

Stressed Out

Let's be honest. For most candidates, making the videos creates the most frustration. Most certificates require two video recordings, although the Music certificate requires three (one for C2 and two for C3). Log onto any National Board internet group or attend almost any candidate support meeting, and you'll find teachers struggling to get a video that "will work." Horror stories about video-taping abound when any group of candidates or NBCTs gather. Getting a workable video segment is paramount because the bulk of Component 3 writing can't be completed until the segment is filmed and chosen. Most teachers tackle Component 3 using these strategies:

- *Plan the Perfect Lesson:* In reality, there is no such thing as a perfect lesson, but candidates never stop trying to film one. It's logical to think that if the lesson is great, the video will be great too. But even a well-planned lesson can't always overcome the glitches that can occur: a disconnected cord, bad sound, a confrontational student, or the first time all year that your students had nothing to say. Filming virtually, if that's what you need to do, also presents additional challenges.

- *Video Early and Video Often:* This makes sense. It can be helpful to film lessons for practice—to get yourself and your students comfortable with the camera. This strategy goes with the premise that if you film lots of lessons, eventually you'll get a segment that "will work." This is the strategy I relied on. I recorded twelve lessons before finally finding a segment for my small-group video. By the end, my students and I were exhausted by the effort. It's one thing to film for practice and another to be clueless about filming. I estimate that it took close to thirty hours of viewing for me to find that magic fifteen-minute segment. If only I'd known then what I know now about the video component, I'd have saved myself a lot of time and stress.

Why Video?

Start by understanding *why* the National Board asks you to do a video component.

- Video recorded teaching sessions offer particularly strong evidence of a candidate's pedagogical knowledge and ability to manage learning opportunities because the videos are snapshots of real lessons in real time.
- Videos allow the candidate to be in charge of what an assessor sees. The assessor sees only what you choose to submit. Did a student get sick? Don't use that part. Surprise fire drill while you are taping? Start over another time. You have the power and flexibility to determine what an assessor sees. Think of the scenario every teacher has experienced when an administrator comes in for his/her observation/evaluation. One just prays it's a "good" day—that everything goes okay because this one shot is all you get. Submitting videos is a gift really, an opportunity to show your real teaching practice on your terms.
- Videos are an excellent way to showcase the climate of a classroom, teaching and management strategies, student engagement, the discourse environment, and the interactions that take place during teaching and learning sequences. Assessors get a real glimpse of your classroom as well as the opportunity to view a snapshot of your teaching and your students' learning. Virtual teaching produces some extra challenges in capturing these elements, but many have done so successfully.
- It's hard to fake a productive learning environment if it doesn't really exist.

Filming Frustrations

Even though the rationale for the video component is powerful, getting one you want to use can be among the most frustrating aspects of the certification process. Why is that?

- Most of us hate seeing and hearing ourselves on video. We don't like our hair, our clothes, our weight, or our voice. We may discover vocal or physical mannerisms we weren't aware of and don't like. So a major obstacle is to get over ourselves. It takes some effort, but you can learn to concentrate on the content of the lesson instead of yourself. Consider it a major milestone when you conquer this hurdle.
- Technology and logistical issues can be frustrating and intimidating. Being unfamiliar with the equipment, arranging for someone to come in and film, figuring out how to film without any help, poor sound quality, and filming virtually all cause angst. Add in cords that come unplugged, dead batteries, and challenging student behaviors, and you have the ingredients for a possible meltdown.

What Works! Video Smart!

The strategies of planning a perfect lesson and taping early and often aren't without merit. Everyone becomes accustomed to the camera and feels more comfortable. Along the way, the logistical and technological challenges become more manageable.

But in truth, and this is what most candidates struggle with, the lesson you submit doesn't have to be perfect. Neither do the students nor the teacher have to be perfect. In fact, a "perfect" video could give the appearance of being staged. The assessors aren't looking for a dog-and-pony show; they expect to see a real lesson. "Dog and pony shows" almost always backfire in some way. "Real lessons" give honest data to write about. I have watched videos where a student is seen asleep, a student displays a certain verboten hand signal, or a special need student vocalizes loudly, non-stop through the whole video—and all those submissions scored well because the teacher wrote well about the situation. The best way to "video smart" is to understand the prompts, learn what the assessors expect to see, plan a lesson that shows the Standards you are asked to demonstrate, and keep the lesson real.

The Video Formats/Configurations

- Two videos, each a maximum of fifteen minutes
- Show two different formats: whole class, small group, pairs, 1:1, or other appropriate grouping
- Show a variety of strategies/activities between the two videos.
- Some certificate areas specify subjects/topics to be addressed. Examples:
    - MCGen/ECGen: science, social studies, and/or math
    - Music: Two lessons from different units of study with a focus on musicianship
    - Physical Education: Two lessons from different units of study with a focus on developing motor skills

The focus for each video varies by certificate area. Read the *What Do I Need to Do* section of your instructions for details that fit your certificate area.

What Works! PLAN BACKWARDS!

Like when planning other components, an effective way to get a video you want to submit is to *plan backwards*. Know your destination, and then plan the route to get there.

- Start with the prompts. Determine what the outcome of the prompt could look like.
- Brainstorm how to show the outcome in light of the goals and NB standards.
- Include as much of the evidence assessors expect to see as possible.

Instead of blindly filming (except when just practicing) and hoping the evidence is there, begin with the prompts and the evidence you need to demonstrate—then plan how to include that evidence. To illustrate the thinking that plays into this strategy, read prompts and hypothetical plans from the *ECGen, Social Studies/History, and English Language Arts* Component 3 certificate areas. The planning process is the same for any certificate. I've written in the first person to model the thinking process a candidate might use.

ECGEN: How did you monitor and assess student progress during the lesson and how did this influence your decision making during instruction? How was student feedback provided and what was your rationale for providing it in this manner?

- I'll do verbal and non-verbal check-ins with individuals and groups.
- I'll ask students to give thumbs-up/thumbs-down signals to check understanding.
- I'll plan a think-pair-share activity and monitor the engagement of each pair by walking around the classroom and stopping to listen to each pair.
- I'll use post-it notes to give specific feedback to individuals and pairs.

AYA:SS/H: What specific approaches, strategies, techniques, or activities did you use to promote active student engagement in the lesson? Cite specific examples from the video recording.

- I'll plan for a quick whole group review on the Yalta Conference.
- I'll arrange small groups to work independently to reach consensus through compromise.
- I'll ask open-ended questions, give wait time, and probe for understanding.
- I'll provide resources to foster students' knowledge of the major points of the Yalta Conference.

EA/ELA: To what extent did you achieve the lesson's goal or goals? Provide evidence from the video recording to support your answer. What were your next steps with these students as a result?

- I'll monitor students' use of time and note how easily they complete the activity within the time frame.
- I'll watch students' body language and engagement, and listen to their comments.
- I'll evaluate students' questions and their ability to respond with thoughtful answers.
- I'll listen for comments indicating understanding—or not.

Now that the hypothetical candidate has notes about what to plan as evidence for each prompt, the lesson can be structured following the

Architecture of Accomplished Teaching. The candidate can be confident there will be evidence to write about for each prompt. In your real classroom, you may discover that your class needs upfront modeling and practice of cooperative learning strategies for example, and/or procedures you expect them to use for the activities *before* filming takes place. The day you film for real, isn't the day to try something new.

What Assessors Expect to See

This is what every candidate wants to know... what are the assessors looking for? It really isn't a secret; the clues are in the instructions. In both videos, show these types of evidence: the goal/objective stated in the writing matches the instruction seen on the video.

- A variety of teaching strategies, techniques, and/or activities are evidenced.
- Teacher-to-student interaction occurs.
- Student-to-teacher interaction occurs.
- Student-to-student interaction occurs.
- Safe, fair, equitable, and challenging learning environment are evident.
- You can cite specific examples from the videos.
- Bullets in the Selecting a Lesson for Each Video, on pages 7 and 8 in most certificates, showcase areas that the assessors will expect to see in the video and in your writing.

What Works! Finding Evidence Assessors Expect to See in a Generalist Video Lesson.

- *The goal matches the activity.* Goal: Students learn about Newton's Laws of Motion (science). Activity: Students roll small cars down ramps covered with various surfaces to test Newton's Laws.
- *Multiple approaches, strategies, techniques, and/or activities are evident.* Some students prepare ramps with various surfaces for an inquiry activity, while others are engaged in snapping together Unifix cubes to use for measurement and gather cars to roll down the ramps; still others write their observations in their science journal. There is choice and/or differentiation of tasks and information is presented in more

than one way: perhaps in the forms of reading text, discussion, and a video.

- *Teacher-to-student interaction*: The teacher engages students in discourse/discussion about the motion of the cars as they roll down the ramp, asks open-ended questions, and asks them to compare, evaluate, explain or defend an answer/approach.
- *Student-to-teacher interaction*: A student question or comment may spark a back-and-forth exchange. The teacher has comments or questions ready to encourage responses and notes misconceptions or interactions that occur that indicate understanding.
- *Student-to-student interaction*: The teacher listens for misconceptions or understandings expressed as students work together. Each member of the group is responsible for part of the inquiry activity.
- *Safe, fair, equitable, and challenging learning environment:* The teacher demonstrates that each student's uniqueness is valued by describing how the differentiated goals, instruction, and assessments meet students' needs. Examples include:
- Providing preferential seating and appropriate assistance.
- Recognizing learning styles, cultural values, and examples of fair play.
- Giving each student the opportunity to do both activities.
- Explaining why students are grouped in a certain way; why the student in the blue shirt uses a spelling device when writing or why only student A was allowed to use a particular tool or technology.

Why These Work!

Making those elements evident in the video provides strong support and evidence, and lends validity to the Written Commentary. The video shows the *what*, the writing explains the *how and why*. It's a reasonable assumption that if the lesson is well planned—for both content and the evidence assessors expect to see—you stand a better chance of creating a segment "that works" without exhausting yourself and your students by filming over and over. You still may need several attempts, but you increase the odds that you won't be trying to get a usable video segment at the last minute or in a panic.

Because the Standards are embedded within the evidence, the video segments that include as much evidence as possible may be ones that will "work." The purpose of the video is to *support* the Written Commentary, so the assessors first read the Written Commentary and Forms, then watch the video to verify the meshing of the two. The videos are not scored separately.

Demonstrating the NB Standards

The NB Standards contain multiple examples to help you plan and recognize evidence in your own practice. At the beginning of each component is a list of Standards that are significant to that component. At each planning step, ask what could occur in the video to show that standard? For example, when students are engaged in a discussion that deepens their understanding, what Standard is evident? When students interact with each other, what Standard is evident? When students are able to make choices, what Standard is evident? When students take ownership of their own learning, what Standard is evident? Often, something in a video will evidence more than one Standard. Appendix Figure 8.1 can help you find and list the evidence in your video.

Looking for Clues in the Instructions and Rubric

Reading the component instructions thoroughly is the only way to identify evidence that assessors expect to see. It's also important to be familiar with the Level 4 Rubric, which explains the 3Cs: *clear, consistent, convincing* evidence. Many specific examples of evidence are included in the explanation of each NB Standard, and incorporating these makes a stronger case for your accomplished teaching. Reading the NB Standards and highlighting specific strategies that are appropriate for your students, at this time, in this setting will move you in the right direction. All of these contain clues about the types of evidence key to each component. For example:

- A prompt asks *how you monitored and assessed student progress during the lesson and how did this influence your decision making during instruction?* Be sure to include one or more examples in your writing.
- General responses are usually not strong evidence. Be specific.
- Use the keywords in the prompt to point to specific examples from the video.

Example from AYA/Math: Group 3 used the decimal approximation of 0.333 for the scale factor instead of using 1/3. As a result, their equation produced outputs that almost matched the data. This was an unintended opportunity I took to discuss the appropriateness of rounding when creating equations. While it was not an intended learning goal, the small group format allowed me to explore this concept with the group to address their learning needs.

What Does Evidence Look Like?

Here are some places to look and listen for evidence/examples in a video. Pay attention to:

- What is said
- What is done
- What questions are asked
- Facial expressions
- Body language
- Level of engagement
- Interactions
- Instructional Materials
- Goals and Objectives
- Strategies
- Assessments
- Teachable Moments

Each of the above is connected to one or more of the Five Core Propositions and hence to one or more NB Standards. If assessors see the above evidence in your video, and if you write about the evidence with specific examples, you will produce a strong product.

What Works! Being Specific!

Citing *specific examples* of evidence is the best way to provide the clear, consistent, and convincing evidence called for in the Level 4 Rubric. The key word is *specific*! Following are some *hypothetical* examples:

- Because I knew that Todd struggled to find the area of a quadrilateral, I gave him a set of centimeter cubes to practice filling the interior spaces of square and rectangular shapes. At the beginning of the video, he uses the cubes to fill the shapes (find the area). Next he draws his own squares on graph paper. At the end of the video, he explains the process to his partner. This showed me that he was catching onto the concept of area so he could soon apply the formula to quadrilaterals.

- The girl in the red sweater repeatedly insisted that insects had eight legs, so I matched her with a compatible partner to read The Wonderful World of Insects *together. Later in the video, she correctly drew an insect with six legs.*

- Group 2 made several unsuccessful attempts to assemble the model. They were arguing, so I approached them and asked what procedure they had followed so far. I asked the group to come up with a strategy that would help them assemble the model without missing any steps. Their solution was to ask Group 3 to show them the steps they had used to complete the model. While watching Group 3, Richard realized that they had not matched the parts correctly and pointed this out to his partners. After that, Group 2 was able to return to their model and complete it successfully.

Why This Works! Specific examples are where evidence is found.

What Works! Choose the Video Segment

- Read the instructions so you are crystal clear about the requirements regarding time, grouping, and editing, for example. Directions must be followed exactly. They are the final word.

- Know the *maximum* number of minutes specified in the instructions.

- A video can be *shorter* than the maximum number of minutes allowed.

- Most videos will be ten to fifteen minutes. A video shorter than ten minutes may not be sufficient to showcase the evidence you want to show.

Watch the entire lesson once to get a sense of its quality. Then, once you have some promising footage, use Appendix Figure 8.1 to analyze and record the evidence you find. Try these strategies to locate a usable segment.

What Works! Watch the Segment Multiple Times

- *Watch the first time* to verify that the goal and objectives in the video are evident and that they match the goal and objectives stated in the Written Commentary and Forms.
- *Watch the second time* with the sound off to watch for body language and facial expressions that indicate student engagement and interactions.
- *Watch the third time* with only sound (turn your back to the screen). Listen for exchanges between the teacher and students, students and the teacher, and student to student, as well as discourse about the content.
- *Watch the fourth time* with your class. The comments they make can be insightful! It's guaranteed that they will notice things you didn't, and you can include these in the analysis and reflection sections. It may also inspire kids to be more engaged.
- Watching the video with colleagues and other candidates is also an effective strategy.

What Works! Document the NB Standards in the Video

Review the video segment for evidence of the NB Standards listed in each component and in the Level 4 Rubric. Note the evidence you find.

- What did you do and say?
- What did the students do and say?
- What interactions took place between people?
- What interactions took place with the content?
- What did you do to promote a climate of learning?
- Are all of the sections in the instructions addressed?
- Did you respond to *all parts* of the prompts and questions?
- Consider choosing a segment not focused on showing directions or transitions because these elements of a lesson may lack evidence.

Let's return to the sample *MCGen/ECGen* scenario described earlier to analyze which NB Standards might be demonstrated by the student-to-student interaction described.

- *The scenario: part of the class participates in an inquiry activity with ramps while the others write in their science journal. Each member is responsible for helping to determine the surface of their ramp. They have all received direct instruction and completed other activities to build foundational knowledge about force and motion. All will have the opportunity to complete both activities.*

Continuing with the MCGen Certificate Standards, here are possible ways the Standards could be evidenced. Note the use of the first person to model the writing style. Using the first person assures that the teacher is visible within the lesson.

Writing about Knowledge of Students:

- *I arranged* groups to address student strengths/needs and assigned jobs within the group to address learning strengths, needs, interests, and language fluency.
- *I presented* instruction, materials, and activities that are age appropriate. They show my knowledge and understanding of how to organize and manage learning.

Writing about Knowledge of Content and Curriculum:

- *I addressed* an important science topic and planned appropriate goals and objectives.
- *I taught* information that was accurate and connected to real life.

Writing about Instructional Decision Making:

- *I planned* a discovery (inquiry) activity and product that fostered inquiry and required students to explain their thinking.
- *I provided* a variety of nonfiction materials to foster reading skills and extend and enrich learning.
- *I asked* students to demonstrate ways the topic applies to real life.

- *I gave* students choices in how they showed their knowledge of the water cycle.
- *I presented* the core knowledge in a variety of ways.
- *I planned* activities to address various learning styles and students' strengths.
- *I used* a variety of assessments to determine student progress.
- *Students showed* their knowledge in various ways, including writing science journals, and making presentations.
- *I evaluated* the success of the unit and planned for the next steps.

Writing about Reflective Practice:

- *I analyzed* the results of the assessments in order to know whether instruction was successful and decide where to go next.
- *I realized* I needed to re-teach the concept of condensation because students had not yet corrected misconceptions.

The above points are examples of how to address and write about the Standards in the Written Commentary and on Forms. Note as well how the Standards connect to the Architecture of Accomplished Teaching.

Finalizing the Details

- Select a segment that demonstrates the *most* evidentiary support and is the richest with the Standards and Level 4 Rubric evidence.
- Find a segment that fits the time frame in the instructions.
- Use a stopwatch or the time stamp for exact time
- List the specific examples you can use as evidence.
- Upload the chosen segment onto your National Board Portal for submission.
- Follow formatting and labeling directions exactly!
- Call 1-800-22TEACH or email with questions. Rely only on your instructions and/or the NBPTS for information!

What Works! Filming the Lesson

The information contained in your NBPTS General Portfolio Directions regarding filming techniques is comprehensive and the definitive word. However, here is a list of additional tips.

- Keep signed permission slips in a safe place for all students and adults being filmed. Those without permission can be seated out of camera range.
- Film using a phone, digital camera, or other device such as an iPad.
- Be sure you can upload your format onto your E-Submission Portal.
- Learn to ignore the camera and teach your students to do the same. If using a digital camera, set the camera up often to practice, but put tape over the on light so that it becomes just another object in the room.
- Consider having a student operate the camera if using a tripod.
- Set the tripod at student eye level, which may mean placing the camera/device on a low table or even the floor.
- Have sturdy extension cords available and use them safely (taped to the floor).
- Use an external microphone with groups if possible. This isn't possible with all devices.
- Consider using a Swivl device for filming. It will "follow" your moves around the room.
- Show the faces of the students and teacher. For stationary filming of a whole group, a camera position in a front "corner" will capture the most faces.
- Show the teacher's face clearly at least every five minutes. The camera should focus mainly on students to showcase their discussion and actions. The teacher can walk in and out of the frame.
- Don't make the video all "teacher talk."
- Don't "stage" any lesson. Forget the "dog and pony" show. "Real" is honest, natural, and gives you real material to write about. "Fake" is unethical and almost always backfires.

- Turn off fans, aquarium pumps, etc. when possible to avoid extraneous noise.
- Pay attention to what you wear. The assessors receive bias training, and dress is often casual, but you still want to appear professional. Think about what might be hanging out, hanging over, or showing when you bend over. Avoid attire with the school name boldly emblazoned on it.
- Allow yourself one "pity party" to moan and groan about your hair, your voice, your weight, or whatever other faults you perceive you have. Then get over yourself so you can focus on the content of the video!
- The biggest video mistakes: The teacher talks too much; not enough student-to-student talk; too much procedural talk; not enough content talk.

More Filming Tips

- Read your directions very carefully so that you know exactly what groupings Component 3 asks for. The instructions are the final word!
- If you have no camera operator, place the camera/device on a tripod near the front, off to one side to film a whole group. You can move the camera whenever needed. You don't need to be visible every minute but your face should show at least every five minutes.
- Carry the camera/device to a location, set it down to capture a group, and walk in and out of the frame if needed. Turn the camera around occasionally to show your face.
- The camera/device can be on a tripod focused on one location, a table for example, and groups can move to and from the table. It's okay to show short transitions.
- Have the camera operator follow you from group to group, but it's permissible for them to also pan the room occasionally or focus on one group for an interval.
- Do everything possible to have student voices heard. It helps the assessors and saves you from needing to do extensive transcription in the writing.

- The video is support for your Written Commentary and doesn't need to be perfect. Plan some logistics for filming, but keep them as simple as possible.

Writing the Video Component: Describe, Analyze, and Reflect

Every component requires three types of writing: description, analysis, and reflection, and each prompt can call for one or more of the three types of writing. The borders between the types can be fuzzy, but keep the following generalities in mind:

- Description is an objective retelling to give the reader a sense of being in the classroom. It answers the questions what and which. Key verbs are describe, state, list, and define.
- *Analysis* reveals the thought processes used to make instructional decisions and explains the significance and impact of the evidence submitted. Analysis involves the interpretation of the facts. Key analysis questions are *why, how* and *so what*. Key verbs are *analyze, explain, because, in order to, and interpret*.
- *Reflection* deals with the thought processes that occur after a teaching situation.

It is hindsight and takes place in order to improve future teaching practices. The key reflection question is *now what?* Reflection cues include *improve, change,* and *in the future*.

Vocabulary in the Video Prompts

- *Learning Environment:* How factors such as the nature of the learning experience, the degree of intellectual risk-taking encouraged by the teacher, respect, fairness, equity, access, and classroom management come together.
- *Student engagement:* The extent to which the students are actively involved in the learning
- *Interactions:* Verbal and non-verbal interactions between the teacher and students, the students and the teacher, and student-to-student.

WHAT WORKS! Write about Evidence in the Video

- The video itself isn't scored, but it's evidence to support the Written Commentary.
- Point out your teaching behaviors. Some, such as questioning strategies, are obvious, while others, like using an attention signal or body language, are more subtle.
- Refer to specific moments and explain what you were thinking when you said a particular thing or took a particular action. Even if an action is obvious, explaining the rationale behind it will make the writing more convincing.
- Describe any adjustments you made during the lesson and tell why.
- Point out any aha moments that occur in student understanding.
- Refer to students using an identifying characteristic, i.e., *the blonde boy*, or by first name.
- Use a time reference (optional) if you have space and feel it will help the assessors find the evidence. *At 7:54, I addressed Tony's misconception that all heavy objects sink.*
- Script the dialogue and use a quote if it is difficult to hear something important: *When the volcano erupted, the boy in the red shirt said, "The liquid spurting out is magma."* However, try not to do this too often, because it consumes valuable space.
- Call attention to student engagement. Remember to include the more subtle signs such as eye contact, body language, posture, and taking notes. Engagement doesn't always have to be active movement or talk.
- Don't discard a video for behavioral reasons alone. It may allow you to discuss challenges you deal with (possibly also mentioned in the Instructional Context), and your rationale for addressing the behavior.
- Use *specific examples* from the video. *Mike was able to borrow successfully when he subtracted.* Make this your mantra!
- State and explain your rationales for the decisions you make and actions you take.

Why These Work!

Presenting evidence in the video component is not about looking a particular way, sounding a particular way, or teaching a particular way. The video is not meant to be a "Hollywood production". It is about showing your teaching practice in an honest way; giving a snapshot of what you really do and how you really teach. It's about how you plan, how you respond, and how you impact student learning using your own teaching style, your understanding of your students, and your pedagogical knowledge. You must specifically point this evidence out in your writing.

Fabricated Writing Examples:

AYA/ Math: At 12:45, Group 5 uses both calculators and their phones to calculate the growth/decay factors and find initial values of the exponential equation they created. Justin shares his findings with his group, but others got a different answer. Logan then leans over Justin's desk and goes over the steps again. This time, Justin's results are correct.

World Languages/French: Each group had a scenario about traveling, and they were to use vocabulary and grammatical structures to check in at a hotel, arrive at the airport, or plan a sight-seeing trip. At 2:21, Group 1 works together to give directions in French to a hotel from the airport. Monique, in blue, creates a map using directional words and place names. She struggles with the pronunciation of the place names and others in her group can be heard correcting her. However the group members also were not saying the place names correctly, so I went to the group and had them echo my pronunciation. As a result, all their pronunciation improved.

EA/ELA: I used a 2-circle Socratic circle as the format for this lesson. To help students who were struggling I encouraged them to look back at their notes from the previous class, so they could find information and be able to participate in the discussion. I do this at 5:16 in the video when the blonde boy in the green shirt was not prepared to speak. I asked him to look back at what he wrote on Friday. As a result he was able to participate in the discussion.

EMC/LRLA: I incorporated differentiation into the graphic organizers by providing varying degrees of information on organizers. At 4:29, Louis, in black, works on a cloze sentence graphic organizer because he needs more teacher assistance. Marie had sentence starters to foster more independent work, while Liz, who works above grade level, had space for taking notes. They talk together about the Thomas Edison video they watched and the cause and effect of his experiments. Stewart asks Marie why Edison had so many failures, and Marie replies "Because he had to try a lot of different ideas to see what worked and what didn't," which shows understanding of cause/effect on Marie's part and helped clarify the concept for Stewart.

ECGen: For the most part, the students raised their hands and waited their turns, which is evidence of the social skill for this lesson. At 6:12 and 6:27 I redirected some the student's attention. There are some occasions when one student talks over another one, like at 6:38 when the girl in the red shirt is talking about Rapunzel; but no one gets upset or verbalizes that it is "their turn".

EAYA/PE: At 42:12, Dan asked what would happen if two people tagged each other simultaneously during the game. This was significant because Dan is often seen as the underdog by his peers. After the game, at 47:00, I complimented him for asking that question. I probed, asking how his peers' reactions made him feel during the game today. He stated, "Good because I think it helped everyone play fair because I asked a question that could solve a problem before it happened."

What Works!

Note the use of the first person and active voice verbs: *I knew; I went; I encouraged; I asked; I do; I incorporated; I redirect; I showed; I probed*. This makes the teacher's intentions clear, keeps the teacher's thinking and actions visible, and uses less space. Specific examples provide strong evidence.

9 Writing for Component 4
Effective and Reflective Practitioner

Six Word Memoir: How does this impact student learning?
DANIELLE, PA

Overview

Component 4 focuses on your ability to use reflection to effectively develop knowledge of your students and apply that knowledge to assessment practices to move their learning forward. You'll also discuss a Professional Learning Need (PLN) you have and a Student Need (SN) that requires collaboration, advocacy, and/or leadership.

You'll gather information from a variety of sources including assessments, colleagues, and families, and collaborate with colleagues and the larger community to impact your students' learning. The information you submit, the sources of this information, and how you use it will be specific to your subject area and the unique characteristics of the students you teach, your school, district, and community. Component 4 also contains 7 Forms, more than any other component. Each addresses one or more elements of the component.

In a nutshell, Component 4 asks you to focus on five elements: (1) your knowledge of students, (2) generation and use of assessments, (3) professional development, (4) participation in learning communities, and (5) collaboration and reflection.

How to Approach Component 4

Many candidates call Component 4 *the bear or the beast*. This is because Component 4 addresses several elements of one's teaching practice rather than having a single focus. As a result, Component 4 can feel disjointed. Here are some strategies to help you organize your thoughts and work, and see the component in full.

- Understand that the Knowledge of Students (KOS) section and the Generation and Use of Assessment section *must* be tightly connected.
- Understand that Professional Learning Needs (PLNs) and the Student Need (SN) *can/may* be connected to the KOS and Assessment sections, *can/may* be connected to each other and/or *can/may* each stand alone. These are your choices to make.
- Think of the Knowledge of Students and Generation and Use of Assessment as one section.
- Think of the Participation in Learning Communities (PLN and SN) as one section.

What Works!

Chunk Component 4 out into sections and work on one section at a time. See Appendix Figure 9.1 for visuals to help you see the Component 4 connections.

Why This Works!

You'll feel less overwhelmed and more in control.

Knowledge of Students (KOS)

The purpose of gathering information about your students is to use that knowledge to plan, teach, and assess a unit of study. To respond comprehensively to the prompts in the KOS section, you'll need specific evidence you've used at least *two* resources. *At least*, means two is the *minimum* number of resources you'll reference. Your Component 4 instructions and National Board Standards contain many examples to spur your thinking. The information you gather for the KOS section must be directly connected to the plans and choices you make in the Assessment section. You'll create a

Group Profile using a group of students you teach. Check your instructions for details applicable to your certificate area.

Generation and Use of Assessment

The prompts in the Assessment section are written to assess your *Assessment Literacy*. Assessment Literacy can be defined as understanding how to use assessment for learning with this group of students, at this time, in this setting. It shows you know how to interpret assessment results, know what makes an effective assessment, and know how to apply assessment information to refine your teaching and maximize student learning.

The Assessments

You'll administer three types of assessments to your Profile Group. Each has a specific purpose and must be tightly connected to 1) the KOS of the Profile Group; and 2) the range and scope of the assessments as a collection. It's imperative to understand each type of assessment and to plan each type based on your knowledge of students and your content area. Only by fostering these understandings will you be able to craft strong responses to the prompts.

The Pre-test/Post-test Dilemma

Although pre-tests share a purpose with a Formative Assessment, to learn what students know about a topic in order to plan instruction, the timing of a pre-test sets it apart from a Formative Assessment. Pre-tests are given *before* any instruction and often include objectives covering an entire unit from beginning to end; a FA is given *during* instruction and addresses a portion of the objectives of a unit. You can certainly give a pre-test if you want, but you wouldn't count it as a Formative Assessment and submit it. If this isn't clear, you may need to research types of assessments to clarify the distinction. Many teachers assess with a pre-test and post-test system. Post-tests meet the definition of a Summative Assessment because they are given at the end of a unit of study, over all the objectives of the unit.

Midterms and Final Exams

Midterm and final exams follow a similar line of thinking. A midterm exam is usually given midway through a learning period, sometimes a unit of study, sometimes a more lengthy period such as a semester or quarter that might include more than one unit of study. For the purposes of Component 4, you could use a midterm exam as the Formative Assessment if it covers learning up to a certain point in a unit of study. Like a post-test, a Final Exam could be considered a Summative Assessment assuming it evaluates only the learning of the unit of study used for Component 4.

Formative Assessment (FA)

Formative assessments are a range of formal and informal evaluative procedures administered *during* the learning process/a unit of study. The purpose is to measure learning *up to a particular point* within a learning experience, in order to determine next steps. A Formative Assessment is given *after* instruction has begun over a specific set of skills and/or objectives. Each candidate submits *one* Formative Assessment for Component 4—no matter how many are actually given within a unit of study. If a candidate gives multiple Formative Assessments, then *one* should be chosen to submit.

Student Self-Assessments (SSAs)

Along with the Formative Assessment, you will submit three Student Self-Assessments. The SSAs must be connected to the *same set of objectives* evaluated on the Formative Assessment, so they are given at approximately the same time. The SSAs may all be the same, or they can be differentiated for various learners.

Self-Assessments encourage students to reflect on their learning experiences. SSAs may include rubrics, reflective questions, or graphic organizers. Self-assessment occurs when students judge their own work and learning in order to improve performance. They allow the teacher to tap into student thinking in order to see how our teaching can better respond to their needs. Feedback and self-assessment can strongly address the fairness, equity, and diversity National Board Standard. Examples of self-assessment might include:

- Rubrics that describe levels of competency
- Three things I learned are ___
- Reflective questions
- Graphic organizers, particularly appropriate for young students/non-readers
- Ticket out of class
- Teacher-student face-to-face conference
- Checklists
- Students choose an appropriate "face" to describe how they feel they've learned a certain skill or concept.
- Teachers may need to conference with or read selections to students who cannot yet read.

Summative Assessment (SA)

The Summative Assessment is the assessment given at the *end* of a unit of instruction to measure learning of all the objectives of the unit. The objectives assessed must match tightly with the objectives taught.

Copyrights

Copyrighted assessments may *not* be submitted. Copyrighted assessments must be *described* on the appropriate, accompanying form. The National Board has no preference as far as scoring goes, whether assessments are teacher-made or copyrighted assessments. It is imperative the copyright guidelines be scrupulously followed.

Participation in Learning Communities

In this section, you'll include information and evidence of your participation in learning communities. You'll describe, analyze, and reflect on how your participation is relevant to you and how it impacts both the students you teach and your teaching practice. You'll explain how your participation in learning communities:

- Impacts how you gather information to inform your instructional and assessment practices.
- Contributes to positive and effective learning changes for your students.
- Addresses a Professional Learning Need (PLN) for yourself and/or your colleagues that you identified as a result of your knowledge of students, either a particular group or a broader population, and assessment practices; this need could be cumulative over time from two years prior to your submission date, but the impact must be from within the current year.
- Addresses a Student Need (SN) you've identified that required advocacy, collaboration, and/or leadership on your part or within a larger learning community. The students can be a particular group or a broader population.

Unpacking the Component 4 Prompts

Work backward! Use the information in the prompts to plan and develop opportunities to collect data about each topic and put the data to work to benefit teachers and students. When you start with the end in mind, you can map out a course of action for each part: Knowledge of Students, Generation and Use of Assessments, Participation in Learning Communities, and Reflection.

Writing Component 4

Using sentence stems that restate the wording/questions in the prompts is the simplest, most effective way to respond comprehensively to each prompt. Doing this assures you'll stay on topic and not wander off on a tangent. It also clearly lets the assessor know which prompt you are answering. You learned to do this in elementary school—before learning more sophisticated methods of written communication. Here are some examples from each of the Component 4 sections.

Knowledge of Students

- *What are some of the trends you identified from the information you gathered from multiple sources? How did you identify or confirm the trends?* Some trends I identified are ___ and ___. I identified (or confirmed) these trends by ___.
- *What other factors did you take into account when analyzing and reflecting on the various sources of information and why?* Factors I took into account were ___ and ___. I took these into account because __.

Generation and Use of Assessment:

- *What steps did you take to ensure the assessment results provided consistent, fair, and accurate information about the students' performance?* I took several steps to ensure consistent, fair, and accurate results about student performance. First, I ___. Next I ___ and finally I ___.
- *How did you support students' use of self-assessment during the unit to achieve the unit objectives?* To support students' use of self-assessment during the unit, I _____.

Participation in Learning Communities

- *How did you identify the area of need for professional learning? What factors or information did you consider in determining how to meet that need? What impact did addressing the professional learning need have on student learning?* Due to the coronavirus, my school implemented virtual learning almost overnight causing me to identify I needed to learn ___. Factors I needed to consider in order to gain the skills I needed included __ and __. As a result of the trainings I took, I was able to ___ which impacted student learning by ___.

What Works!

Restating wording in the prompts is the surest way of directly addressing what each prompt asks for.

Why This Works!

Restating the prompt keeps you on topic and increases the chances you'll write a direct and evidence-based response.

Component 4 Forms

Component 4 has more forms than any other component. It's important they all be completed. The forms provide background information and other details not asked for in the prompts. There can be some overlap between information on the forms and information in the Written Commentary, but you shouldn't be strongly repeating yourself. The forms are not scored separately. They are part of the holistic scoring of the component. The Written Commentary, the forms, and evidence submitted all contribute to the final score.

Component 4 Wrap-up

Component 4 has more "moving parts" than most of the other components. Some parts *must* be connected. Some parts *may* be connected or *may* stand alone. Chunk out the sections to make tackling Component 4 more manageable. Use the graphic in the Appendix H as a reference.

10 Component 1 Writing at the Assessment Center

Six Word Memoir: Much to say, so little time.
SAMANTHA, NY

Show What You Know: The Purpose of the Assessment Center Exercises

While Components 2, 3, and 4 are all about your teaching practice— what *you do* - the Component 1 Assessment Center exercises examine what you know about your content as outlined in the National Board Standards.

The Component 1 exercises have evolved since their inception. Originally, this examination portion of National Board Certification lasted an entire day and consisted of eight timed constructed response tests. Currently the assessment has a Selected Response section and a Constructed Response section, lasts four hours, and covers a teacher's knowledge of content and/or pedagogical knowledge. Being an accomplished teacher implies mastery of your disciplinary content, so the Assessment Center exercises:

- Focus on knowledge of *content and curriculum* across facets of your discipline.
- Focus on themes, ideas, and principles that represent core concepts and curriculum within a discipline.
- Ask you to demonstrate content knowledge with responses to three exercises developed and designed by practicing professionals in your certificate area.
- Cover the entire age range of the certificate.
- Allow you to show knowledge of developmentally appropriate content across the full spectrum of your certificate.

The Nature of the Exercises and the Prompts

The nature of the exercises and prompts in the Component 1 exercises varies among certificates, but follows some general patterns. All demand knowledge of content; some also link content knowledge to pedagogy. Math is the only certificate where pedagogy is not included. Component 1 consists of two types of exercises, *Selected Response Exercises* and *Constructed Response Exercises*.

Selected Response Items

Selected Response is the fancy National Board term for multiple choice. Each certificate has forty to forty-five items, five of which are being "piloted" for future exams and do not count in the score. Other features of the Selected Response exercises include:

- Each is labeled with the NB Standard being assessed.
- Each exercise is written as a scenario.
- Four responses are offered for each prompt.
- Items cover a variety of topics and the entire age range of each certificate.
- 8 sample exercises followed by an answer key.

What Works!

Make a list of the topics covered in the samples. Study those topics—they'll be topics you'll encounter on your assessment. Choose the responses you think are the correct choices. If you miss any, do some research on the topics. Ask yourself *why* the National Board chose that response as the correct one. Often, the correct response is the one most student-centered.

Constructed Response Items

This is the "essay" part of the assessment. Here, you'll construct responses to three exercises, each representing a scenario that could occur within a teaching context or, in the case of the math certificate, to solve problems. All exercises in this section follow the same structure:

- Each is labeled with the NB Standard being assessed.
- Each is organized in the same way: Introduction, Criteria for Scoring, Directions, Scenario/Stimulus, Bullets showing What You Must Address, Leveled Rubrics.
- Covers the entire content and age range of your certificate area.

Certificate-Specific Examples

EC/MC Generalist; EC/MC Literacy; Reading/Language Arts; EC/YA Exceptional Needs Specialist: These certificates link content to pedagogy. Knowing *how* to teach the concept *is* the content. The exercises ask the candidate to:

- Analyze student responses to a stimulus/topic.
- Analyze, identify, and interpret student misconceptions/errors about a topic.
- Describe thorough, detailed, and appropriate instructional strategies and materials to correct misconceptions and/or extend understanding of the topic.
- Plan worthwhile goals and a developmentally appropriate instructional sequence based on the Architecture of Accomplished Teaching that will accomplish the goals.
- Integrate another subject into the instruction.
- Provide a thorough, detailed, and appropriate rationale to justify decisions.

AYA/Science; AYA/Mathematics; EA/Social Studies-History: These certificates have exercises that emphasize connections between specialty areas and another context within the discipline as well as your breadth of knowledge across the disciplines. Pedagogy is less important than your depth and breadth of content knowledge.

- Science certificates allow candidates to choose their path of specialty.
- Math certificates have exercises that address specific areas including algebra, calculus, discrete mathematics, geometry, statistics and data analysis, and technology.

- The Social Studies-History certificate asks you to demonstrate the breadth of your knowledge using graphics and documents in the areas of US History, World History, Political Science, Economics, and Geography.
- EA certificates may contain more pedagogy.

World Languages:

- Candidates use a separate room at the Assessment Center suitable for the oral component that is recorded on a computer.
- Candidates compose answers in a separate response booklet.

Music:

- Candidates choose a specialty area of band, orchestra, or vocal music.
- Exercises are geared to a performing area.
- Some exercises feature aural material.
- Some exercises require candidates to write musical notation in a lined response booklet provided at the Assessment Center.

These are just a few examples to illustrate the variety of the exercises/prompts found in various certificate areas. The *Component 1* instructions document contains detailed information about the prompts for each certificate. The samples given are *retired* prompts, meaning they are exercises used in past assessments, but won't be the same ones used in your assessment. The Component 11 instructions are crucial for your preparation for the Assessment Center exercises. Another important and overlooked document is called *Component: Content Knowledge, Assessment Center Policy and Guidelines.* Here you'll find many additional details about preparing for the Component 1 Assessment.

What Works!

Make your own nutshells for the Constructed Response exercises in your certificate area. This will break the prompts into bite-sized chunks that will make it easier to frap what you'll be asked to do in each exercise.

Table 10.1 Selected Assessment Center Exercise Nutshells

Certificate	Exercise	Stimulus	Scoring Criteria
ECGEN	#2 Mathematics	Math problem w/error	Identify misconception/difficulty Identify underlying concept needed Describe one instructional strategy Describe materials/resources Provide rationale for choices
MCGEN	#1 Reading Skills	Transcript of student's oral reading	Identify one strength, one weakness Plan two strategies to address errors Provide rationale for each choice
ECMC/LRLA	#2 Writing Development	Student Writing Sample	Identify one strength/one weakness Describe one effective strategy to build on strength Describe one area of need Describe one strategy to address area of need
AYA/Science knowledge needed Explain how connected to another area of science	#2 Contexts in Science (Biology)	Topic Studied in Biology	Discuss scientific event/discovery Discuss science Describe two effects of the event/discovery on society

Why This Works!

Once you know how to deconstruct the exercises, you'll have a deeper understanding of what each exercise requires. Then you'll be able to look for resources to refresh your memory of topics you don't teach or haven't taught in a while.

More What Works!

Notice that the prompts are multi-part. A common error at the Assessment Center is not scrolling through the entire list of prompts, thus leaving a prompt unanswered. An unanswered prompt earns no score, so pay particular attention to this detail. Other elements of the prompts to pay attention to:

- Each begins with an active verb: *identify, plan, design, connect, describe, cite, provide,* telling exactly what you must do to show your knowledge of content and/or pedagogy.
- Each connects to one or more steps in the Architecture of Accomplished Teaching

The **Criteria for Scoring** rubric included in the Introduction section for each exercise, explains the *level* evidence you must provide. Your response must show clear, consistent, and convincing evidence of each part of the prompts.

Writing Strategies for Component 1 Constructed Response Exercises

- Start with the main ideas, then go back and fill in details.
- Start by restating the question as the beginning of your response.
- Using bullets is okay because space is unlimited—no page limits.
- Match your responses to the prompts. If asked for two goals, write two goals in your response, no more, no less. You get no bonus points for adding more, and time is of the essence.
- Emphasize the NB Standards, student achievement, appropriate choices, and real-world application.

- Skip writing introductions and conclusions. They use valuable time and contain no evidence.
- Use facts and statistical details you know to be true and back them up with evidence.
- Cite examples. Illustrated evidence is strong evidence.
- Formulate and utilize cause and effect information where appropriate. This exemplifies higher reasoning skills
- Be firm in your opinions. Avoid, *I think* . . . or *It may be possible*. Such phrases weaken the discussion.
- Include rationales. Rationales are powerful analyses.
- Respond to every part of the prompts. Omitting information earns no points.

More Strategies for Success at the Assessment Center

- Study! Refresh your knowledge with current information in your content area by reading journals, textbooks, and teacher manuals that span the age spectrum of your certificate.
- Secondary teachers may find retired Advanced Placement/PRAXIS test prompts useful.
- Use the Assessment Center Pearson Vue Tutorial found in the Scoring Guide. This will provide valuable practice and familiarize you with procedures.
- Know the steps on the Architecture of Accomplished Teaching and be able to apply them to lesson planning. SSTARS is an acronym for steps on the AAT.
- Make up your own prompts for additional practice.
- Try practicing with different age groups within your certificate area.
- Analyze the exercise directions. Pay attention to these elements:
  Content Area: Reading, math, science, social studies etc.
  Prompt Materials: A scenario, a stimulus piece, a document
  Action Words: Identify, cite, describe, provide a rationale
  The Task: Show knowledge of . . . , analyze student errors, and give examples of . . .

- Scroll down first! Don't spend the entire time responding to one prompt only to find there are other parts you've missed.
- Read the *whole* exercise. There are often several parts to it—each requiring a response.
- Budget your time. Thirty minutes per prompt.
- Practice responding to prompts using a timer set for Thirty minutes. Keep practicing. You'll get faster each time. This will help you adjust to responding to a timed test.
- Answer each exercise/prompt completely before moving on. Address all of the parts.
- Once you click on *submit*, you cannot return to the exercise. Unanswered prompts earn no points!
- Use the Level 4 Rubric for each exercise. Study the rubric and be sure you understand each and every word in it. Construct your responses to satisfy the Level 4 Rubric.

What Works! Writing Strategies for Success

- Start with the main points, then go back and fill in details.
- If you get stumped, restart by restating the question as the beginning of your response to jog your memory.
- Using bullets is ok—there are no page limits to constrain your space.
- Match the prompts with your answers. If the prompt asks for goals, your response must have goals.
- Emphasize standards, student achievement, and real-world applications where valid.
- Skip introductions and conclusions. You do NOT have to write in paragraphs.
- Include factual and/or statistical details you know to be true and accurate.
- Cite examples where you are able. Illustrated evidence is strong evidence.
- Formulate and utilize cause and effect information where possible. This exemplifies higher-level reasoning skills.

- Be firm in your opinions. Don't say "I think . . ." or "It may be possible . . ." Phrases like these weaken the discussion.
- Write what you already know and address possible misconceptions.

Why These Work!

Knowing what to expect, how to prepare, and how to write responses will lower your anxiety and boost your confidence. You'll do better if you feel ready.

What Works! More Tips for Component 1 Success

- Consider taking Component 1 after you've completed at least one other component. The writing etc. you do on other components will help prepare you to do your best on Component 1.
- Take the Component 1 exercises when you feel you are ready—any time after April 1. Many candidates share that if they give themselves some time off after submission of other components, they have a block of time to focus on preparing and feel less frazzled and more confident.
- Choose and confirm a date as early as you can after getting the testing authorization code the National Board will send to you. This will give you the greatest choice of dates and will help with your long-range planning.
- Confirm your appointment at least a week ahead of time.
- Read all instructions in the *Component 1: Content Knowledge, Assessment Center Policy and Guidelines* carefully so you will know exactly what to take: ID, authorizations, supplies, etc.
- Dress in layers in case the room is hot or cold and do take the breaks offered.
- Take a test drive to the assessment center ahead of your testing day. It will give you peace of mind to know where you are going and how long it will take to get there.

- Take the tutorial offered on Pearson Vue before starting the testing. It will familiarize you with the format and layout of the screen. Especially practice scrolling—as each exercise contains several prompts and you may need to scroll down to see all of the parts.

Why These Work!

With purposeful planning, you can approach Component 1 with confidence. Use what you already know about accomplished teaching practices to show what you know about your subject-specific content.

What Works! Using Assessment Center Resources

- www.nbpts.org has many resources including certificate Standards, scoring rubrics, the *Component 1: Content Knowledge, Assessment Center Policy and Guidelines* document, and the sample exercises in the *Component 1 Instructions*. These provide important information to help you prepare. You can also access the Pearson Assessment Center tutorials and information from this site.

Why This Works!

Using National Board resources will broaden your understanding of Component 1's intent and content—all the better to prepare you to do your best.

11 Candidate Care

Six Word Memoir: How did I gain 20 pounds?
SUSAN, KY

Take Care of Yourself

If you are reading this at the beginning of your candidacy, you may wonder why there is a chapter devoted to this topic. If you are well into your candidacy or near the end, you may now recognize the need to take care of yourself and wish you had realized or admitted it sooner. Going through the National Board Certification process is labor-intensive, time-consuming, and brain challenging—factors that can take a toll on your mental and physical well-being. But no matter where you are in the process, it's never too late to take positive action.

Gain the Gift of Time

Doing some groundwork early in your candidacy can save much stress and frustration later. Your most precious resource will be time: time to think, time to plan, time to write.

What Works!

Here are the top four ideas that can ferret out the valuable time you'll need:

- Ask for support from your family. Delegate some jobs you've always done yourself. Can the kids fold the laundry and change their own beds? Can your spouse regularly take the kids on an outing during a weekend afternoon so you can have an uninterrupted block of writing time? Can someone other than you be responsible for keeping the house picked-up? Can you assign each person one room? Could your significant other help with the grocery shopping or bathe the baby?

- Ask for support at school. Ask your principal to let you off the hook from serving on time-consuming major committees. Most candidates are active members of their school community and often take leadership roles that are time-consuming. Too many meetings will eat away at the time you need for planning and writing your components. Explain you will need fifty to seventy-five hours per component beyond the school day to work on your components and being excused from committees would be an amazing help. Promise you'll be back!

- Find a National Board support group, cohort, or buddy. Make meeting with other candidates a priority. Join a support group and attend regularly if such cohorts are offered in your district. You'll have an NBCT facilitator who can guide you through the process and you'll meet other candidates you can work with, share with, and sympathize with. And they can do the same for you . . . *it's a you scratch my back and I'll scratch yours* kind of symbiotic arrangement that is mutually beneficial. Look at surrounding districts if there is no formal cohort in your district. I've never heard of a cohort who turned down someone who wanted to participate. Most groups meet monthly, so even if it involves a drive, it will likely be worth the effort.

- Find a buddy—a fellow candidate in your district or one who lives near enough to meet with periodically. To find one, look up National Board Certification in your state and ask for a list of candidates or look at the NBCTs listed for your state on the National Board website. Find buddies and an online cohort on any of several Facebook pages. Just a word of caution: *Be very cautious about sending your work to someone you don't know!* If someone plagiarizes your work, there could be negative consequences for both you and the plagiarizer.

- Find at least one weekend or extended period of time every month when you can have uninterrupted work time. Just once, plan to give yourself a working retreat—especially in February, March, or April. If someone you know has a cabin or beach house, ask if you can use it. Rent a room at a hotel. Send your family out of town for a weekend so you can have the house to yourself. Be creative in finding a way to carve out some extra precious time. Sometimes this can work with a buddy, but only if you can limit conversation and concentrate on your own needs.

Why These Work!

These strategies are proven to boost your efficiency, give you the gift of time, and give you the support and resources you'll need.

Procrastination: Your Worst Enemy

I alluded to this earlier, but procrastination is seriously the worst judgment error you can make as a National Board Candidate—*seriously*! It will do you in faster than most people can lick an ice-cream cone on a summer day. Many believe they do their best work under pressure. This may actually be true for one or two out of a hundred candidates. But the other ninety-eight who think they work best under pressure are almost always mistaken—at least in this case. Writing a National Board component is time-intensive and cannot be accomplished by pulling an all-nighter—or even two or three. Candidates who score well have usually devoted weeks if not months to planning and writing a component. They plan and video multiple lessons. They write and revise components multiple times.

As an NBCT who has facilitated literally hundreds of candidates, I can tell you firsthand, procrastination is a devastating habit. It would take many hands to count the number of candidates I've seen who put off reading their Standards, put off reading the instructions, put off planning lessons that met the requirements, put off collecting student work samples, put off filming lessons, and put off writing. I've had candidates who admitted in March they hadn't read their Standards yet, hadn't read their component instructions yet, nor made a single video. Those candidates rarely certified on their first attempt. There is just no way to produce the quality work the National Board expects if one repeatedly and consistently procrastinates.

The fact that I've devoted nearly a full page of text to procrastination should tell you how seriously I regard this as a fatal flaw. You can be the best teacher at your school, but if you don't devote the time and energy to planning and writing, your chances of certifying are slim. There are many reasons teachers don't certify on their first attempt, but please don't let *procrastination* be the reason you don't certify. It is an avoidable pitfall.

What Works! Activate! Don't Procrastinate!

Procrastination is inaction. The best thing you can do is to take action—any action. Taking action has many benefits that serve you well as you work through the process and it can save you at the end.

Be Proactive

What does being a proactive National Board Candidate mean? It means you don't worry and stew for weeks or months before actually doing the things that need to be done. Consider:

- Read your Standards often and really well. Highlight the examples given in each one to refer to later. NBCTs always tell candidates to read their standards thoroughly and often, and there is a reason for that. You have to know them and show them to certify. Your National Board Standards are your Answer Book!
- Read your component instructions often and really well. You can't produce lessons that will meet the requirements unless you truly know what the components ask you to do. Ninety-nine percent of what you need to know and do is in your instructions and your Standards. Period! Get intimate with these documents!
- Get started on *something*. Find one thing in one component to start working on. Once you get the ball rolling, it's more likely you'll keep going. The Instructional Context can be a good starting place. Or respond to one prompt—do anything to get started.
- Start writing early. An instructional context is a good place to start.
- Get a system in place to organize your components and materials. Being able to lay your hands on something when you need it will be an enormous help as you go along.
- Set aside a designated work time each week. Stick to it and use it.

Why These Work!

Proactive behaviors will keep you on track, raise your confidence level, and produce results that pay off. Think of yourself as a sculptor chipping away little by little at the marble. Eventually the sculptor's chipping brings into being a beautiful statue. By chipping away steadily section by section in your instructions, you will produce a fully formed, thoughtful components that documents your accomplished teaching.

Pay Attention to Your Health

As I mentioned in this chapter's opening paragraph, the National Board Certification process is labor-intensive, time-consuming, and brain challenging. All of these things take a toll on the body, mind, and spirit especially as the deadline approaches. But there are things you can do to minimize the effects all this hard work can heap on you.

Your Body

- *Eat right and stay hydrated*. I know . . . yada, yada, yada. You hear this all the time. But considering that you may be doing more sitting than usual at the computer, keeping the carbs and sugar consumption under control could make a difference in the way you feel. Keep a bottle or glass of water handy at the computer and drink it!
- *Exercise*—take some walks. Again, yada, yada, yada . . . but this is another thing that can make a difference. Fit in some short walks, alone if possible. Walking seems to get the juices flowing . . . to your muscles and your brain. I practically wrote some components in my head while on walks. I seemed to be able to think more clearly and figure out how to get past blocks I was experiencing. Outdoor walks worked best for me when the weather permitted . . . maybe the noise at the gym competed with the "noise" in my head. And sometimes I didn't want the hassle of going to the gym. Just heading out my door and walking through the neighborhood was what I found most helpful.
- *Exercise at your computer*. As you get into writing, you'll spend hours sitting and typing. Learn some chair exercises and yoga stretches you can do every 30 minutes or to stretch your neck, shoulder, arm and wrist muscles. They take so little time yet feel so good and will help prevent a lot of aches and pains. Look for *chair and yoga exercises*

on Google or YouTube and find lots of choices. Another strategy is to move your computer to a counter area so you can stand while working rather than sitting. Standing is more beneficial than sitting. Try it! You will feel so much better, I guarantee.

Your Mind

All of the above will help your state of mind, but try these as well.

- *Positive self-talk* can work wonders. To combat those feelings that you are going crazy, you are overwhelmed, and/or this is too hard, formulate some positive statements to help you relax. Try incorporating these thoughts into your mindset:
  - I can figure this out.
  - I'm doing my best.
  - I'll come back to this later.
  - I'll answer just one prompt now.
  - I know how to do this.
  - This is a common feeling for candidates to have.
  - I'm not alone in this process.
  - I'll slow down and approach one prompt/section at a time.
  - I'll read the directions one more time.
  - I'll read this Standard again.
  - I'll ask my buddy, mentor, cohort, or website for support.
  - I can adjust my schedule for just today/this week/until this component is done.

Your Spirit

Taking care of your physical and mental needs will automatically lift your spirits. As you encounter obstacles, you'll find yourself more resilient and able to rebound. You can recognize that tackling a difficult challenge always involves setbacks and frustrations, but you won't let them derail your efforts. You'll be able to continue on in a more positive frame of mind.

What Works!

Planning to care for yourself will help you have the energy you need. You'll have the confidence, stamina, and perseverance to see the challenge through to the end.

Why This Works!

Your body will find a way to take a break one way or another. It's much better for *you* to plan the breaks your body will take rather than find yourself ill, hurting, and unable to work. As a teacher, you are already exposed to massive doses of germs from your students, so do all you can to keep yourself healthy—in body, mind, and spirit!

12 Confusing Topics and FAQs

Six Word Memoir: A PhD without the Stat Class.
CLAUDIA-OK

What Does This Mean?

Every year and in every certificate area, candidates seem to struggle with similar sets of challenges within the process. Especially as the May deadline approaches, websites and Facebook pages that focus on National Board Certification light up with frantic requests for clarification. Part of the issue stems from the language in the portfolio directions. Prompts are written to give candidates the broadest range of possibilities, which is a double-edged sword. It means both that there are fewer limitations placed on pedagogy, for example. But the lack of specificity may contribute to difficulty deciphering what the National Board wants. Some terms used are National Board jargon and may not be familiar to all. And finally, the prompts are often long and contain multiple parts that must be addressed. Here are the topics that candidates bring up again and again, along with *made-up* examples to clarify each.

Overarching Goal, Goal(s), Major Idea, Objectives, and Activities

- **Overarching Goal:** Some certificates have one or more prompt(s) that ask you to explain these elements of your lesson sequence plan. This is the biggest idea, concept, or understanding you want students to take away from the unit of study. It is something that can cut across a variety of areas of a topic and may be difficult to measure. It's like an "umbrella" idea that connects to the goals, objectives, and activities within a unit of study. *Social Studies Example: The students* *will understand that there are a variety of ways to organize and interpret information about people, places, and environments.*

- **Goal:** This is another broad understanding of a topic, but slightly more specific than the overarching goal. It is still conceptual; the learning may be difficult to measure, and it is often articulated with the word *understand*. *Example: The students will understand maps interpret physical and man-made features.* The verb used in goal statements often comes from one of the higher levels of Bloom's Taxonomy and will be more conceptual than concrete.

- **Objective:** The objective describes the specific, measurable learning(s) you want to occur within a particular lesson. *Example: The students will identify physical and man-made features on a map.* The verb(s) used in the objective statement may come from one of the lower levels of Bloom's Taxonomy, is relatively concrete, and articulates a student action to be taken. The learning of objectives can be evaluated/measured.

- **Activity:** This is what the students do to learn/practice the objective. *Example: Students will construct/draw a map that includes physical and man-made features.* When the activity is completed, the teacher will be able to assess whether or not students learned the objective. Notice the concrete, active voice verb used to construct the statement. Be careful not to plan a lesson sequence/unit of study based mainly on activities. It is important that the goals and objectives are planned first. Plan the activities last. Otherwise the goal(s) and objective(s) may not be tightly connected.

Instructional Context and Contextual Information

The very names of these documents guarantee a mix-up. They are like kissing cousins—which is which? They have elements in common but aren't really the same.

- **Instructional Context:** This is about your class. This is the first section of your Written Commentary in Component 2. It gives the assessor a snapshot of your class and your teaching situation (context). Conditions and students you highlight here need to be referenced again in the Written Commentary. Components 3 and 4 use an Instructional Context Form. While the questions may be the same/similar for all Instructional Contexts, your responses may or may not be identical if you are addressing a different subject for each component or a different aspect of your subject for each.

- **Contextual Information:** This document/form is about your school and possibly your district. Here you describe any special programs you teach under, state mandates, type of community your school/district is located in and your access to technology. You need one for each component 2, 3, and 4 and if your work features students from more than one school, you'll need one for each school.
- **Instructional Materials:** Instructional Materials (IMs) are items used or produced during a teaching sequence. They allow assessors to better understand the activity in your video or Written Commentary. They are not scored separately but are considered a part of your component submission. They may be submitted in the same form in which they are presented to the class. Choose Instructional Materials that help the assessor know about the teaching you did, the content you covered and/or enrichment or remediation—things that help the assessor to gain a more complete picture of your lesson.

Formatting and Editing

Both of these figure large in producing your final component copies. Page limits demand clear, concise writing, which is always a challenge. You cannot exceed the page limits. At the end of the maximum number of pages allowed, the assessors simply stop reading. It is a good idea to stick as closely as possible to the suggested page limits give for each section of a component. The National Board knows approximately how much space in needed for well-crafted responses. If you write far less or far more, you are probably either leaving out important evidence or adding fluff. Check the Appendix for a list of editing tips to save space.

- **Formatting:** Your component instructions give very specific formatting specifications that must be followed exactly. The basics include using 12 point, Ariel font, double-spacing and 1 inch margins.

But each certificate and each component may have particular specifications. So my best advice is to read and re-read those instructions. There can be issues such as margins that print with 1 inch borders on one printer but not another to deal with. Also note whether Google Docs and Word documents format your writing the same. There can be differences between the programs.

- **Editing:** Most candidates start the writing process by writing everything they can think of, the natural consequence of which is that some serious editing needs to take place. Here are tips for editing:
  - Use active voice verbs. Eliminate -ing forms and helping verbs. *plan, create...*
  - Use "I" in statements with an active verb. *I organized... I taught*
  - Indent paragraphs 2 or 3 spaces instead of 5 spaces. OR use no paragraphs at all. **Bold** the first word or two of sentences that begins new responses.
  - Use 1 space between sentences.
  - Eliminate "*that, the, this, and my*" as often as possible. This rarely changes the meaning of the sentence.
  - Turn on automatic hyphenation. You can fit more words onto a page.
  - Turn off widows and orphans, which eliminates single lines at the bottom of a page.
  - Start your text on the same line as a heading. *Instructional Context: The class featured in this component...*
  - Don't repeat yourself. Saying something once is enough.
  - Eliminate adjectives and adverbs where possible.

Other Confusing Terms

National Board terminology is often different that the everyday terms used by teachers across the country and that often leads to confusion. The following terms are found in the *General Portfolio Instructions* document:

- **Instructional/Lesson Sequence:** A series of related lessons and/or activities that support a common goal or theme. It is not limited to a single lesson or activity. Example: A lesson sequence on force and motion.

- **Unit:** Part of an academic course focusing on a selected theme or concept. A unit may also refer to a chapter in a curriculum text.
- **Featured Lesson:** The lesson shown in a video or from which student work samples were derived.
- **Evidence:** Accomplished teaching examples or student actions that have a strong foundation in fact, would be convincing to most people, and would not be easily disproved by interpretation. Assessors want to know that you recognized evidence and used it in your teaching. Example: When he said . . . , I knew that he misunderstood the concept. So I referred him back to the graphic organizer. I knew she had trouble tracking print left to right so I . . .
- **Small Group Discussion:** Used in videos to show how a teacher facilitates interactions among students. Generally, it is a group of 3-5 students although the numbers may vary according to specific component directions.
- **Whole-Class Discussion:** Used in videos to show the teacher effectively engaging the entire class as a group. There should be evidence of interactions with individual students but not every student. However it should be clear that the whole class is actively engaged in the discussion.

National Board Certification Is Rigorous Professional Development

National Board Certification is meant to be a rigorous process that takes deep thinking and broad knowledge to accomplish. Every certificate has particular challenges, but the entire process challenges teachers to formulate effective learning *for these students, at this time, in this setting*. It is rigorous professional development in the highest form.

Appendix A

Ten Commandments for Survival as a National Board Candidate

THOU SHALT:

I. Read Thy Directions and Pay Attention to All Details Contained Therein! Know formatting requirements and page requirements.

II. Make Thy Videos Early! When you signed on for this gig, you didn't realize you'd need to become an overnight "Steven Spielberg." Plan your videos to show the elements the assessors are looking for.

III. Thou Shalt Not Procrastinate! Work steadily and don't put off until tomorrow what you can do today. Procrastination is your worst enemy in this process.

IV. Thou Shalt Save Everything! Promise yourself that you will never turn off your computer without backing up and dating all of your work.

V. Learn that Verbs are Thy Friends! Use the active voice and analytical and reflective verbs that will help you respond to the prompts.

VI. Learn that Adjectives and Fluff are Thy Enemies! These are space-hogs and don't add evidence. Stick to a spare, text-book style writing style.

VII. Seek Out Others to Critique Thy Components and Bruise Thy Ego Because They Will Heal Thy Writing! Ask others to read your entries to be sure your writing is clear, consistent and convincing. Getting feedback can lead to better scores.

VIII. Complete your Electronic Submission Before the Deadline Date! Uploading and submitting take longer than you might imagine, so allow plenty of time!

IX. Prepare for Component 1 as Soon as Thou Submits other Components! Heave a sigh of relief at finishing your portfolio, then get ready to demonstrate your content knowledge by reviewing materials that span the age range of your certificate.

X. Bask in the knowledge that Thou Art Among the Minority of Teachers Who Attempt National Board Certification! You have completed a remarkable journey that fewer than 10% of all teachers even attempt, let alone finish. Give thyself a well-deserved pat on the back!

Appendix B
Ten Editing Tips to Trim Space without Trimming Content

1. **Turn off "widow/orphan" control.** This prevents a single line of a paragraph from being at the top of a new page. You'll save several lines in the space of an entry.
2. **Set to auto-hyphenate.** This will break words at the ends of lines to properly hyphenate. Saving even a few spaces on each page can help.
3. **Use contractions.** They save several spaces each time you use them. Word has an auto-correct feature called "Find and Replace". You may need to do this for each contraction.
4. **Use numerals instead of words.** You can break the rule you learned in school. Use numerals such as 12 instead of twelve and 6th instead of sixth.
5. **Start your commentary on the same line as the heading.** Example: Video Analysis: This lesson features eighty-nine first graders learning to sharpen pencils.
6. **Make sure your candidate number is in a header, not in the body.**
7. **Find and replace the period-double-space.** This is a big space saver over the length of a component.
8. **Take *the, my, and that* out of most sentences.** The meaning won't change, but you'll gain space.
9. **Remove as many adjectives and adverbs as possible: Replace: She writes with vivid and inspired word choice . . . with She writes with strong word choice . . .**
10. **Eliminate paragraphs. B**old the first word or two of each new **response** as a visual aid to the assessor. If you use paragraphs, indent 2 or 3 spaces instead of the usual 5 spaces.

Appendix C
Sentence Stems for Analytic and Reflective Writing

- I chose ___ because ___.
- The rationale behind my decision was ___.
- Because I know ___, I ___.
- The __ on his paper showed me ___, so I ___.
- First I ___, then I followed up by ___.
- This was significant because ___.
- When I saw ___, I realized ___.
- In order to ___, I ___.
- The reasons I chose ___ were ___.
- I used a variety of strategies including ___, ___, and ___.
- I saw the error was caused by ___, so I ___.
- As a result of ___, Jennifer was able to ___.

Appendix D
Component 3: Analysis of a Video

Minute	Teacher Talk	Student Talk	Interaction S/S S/T T/S	Evidence of Prompt/ Rubric Bullet
1:00				
2:00				
3:00				
4:00				
5:00				
6:00				
7:00				
9:00				
10:00				
11:00				
12:00				
13:00				
14:00				
15:00				
			Students to student Students to teacher Teacher to student	

Appendix E
Video Tips for Component 3

Below are some tips for analyzing the Component 3 videos. Candidates respond to the same prompts twice—once for each video.

Candidates need to understand:

- Each video shows a separate lesson.
- Each video highlights a different instructional format (whole/large group; small group/other). More than one format can be evident on a single video, but ONE must be clearly dominant.
- Each video must capture evidence of your teaching practice (instruction), learning environment, and student engagement.

When analyzing a video, look for these elements:

- In the "Selecting a Video" section (pages 7 & 8 in most certificate directions) are a set of bullets addressing the areas of learning environment, student engagement, and instruction.
- Find as many examples of these bullet points as possible—both in the video(s) and in the writing. Some will be overt: words spoken, questions asked, room arrangement, resources, on-topic, academic discussion, etc. Others will be more subtle: tone of voice, body language/eye contact, on task behaviors, etc.
- The more examples found, the better. Points not visible in the video(s), but evident in the lesson, should be referenced in the writing.
- Two prompts in the Written Commentary directly ask candidates to cite evidence from the video. The video segment chosen MUST show those examples.

Important Questions:

- What is the goal of the lesson?
- What instructional format(s) is shown on the video(s)?
- What examples of each bullet point are evident in the video(s)?
- What evidence/examples can you cite from the video(s) as responses to the prompts that ask directly for examples from the video(s)?

Appendix F
SSTARS Lesson Plan Template Based on the Architecture of Accomplished Teaching

STUDENTS (Step 1: Knowledge of Students) WHAT I KNOW ABOUT: • These students at this time, in this setting • Learning styles • Abilities • Needs • Prior Knowledge	
SET GOALS (Step 2: Set high, worthwhile goals) • Goals • Objectives • Activities • Unifying Concepts/Big Ideas	
TEACH (Step 3: Implement instruction) • Appropriate strategies • Activities support goals • Appropriate pacing	
ASSESS (Step 4: Evaluate learning in light of the goals) • Monitor progress purposefully • Assess throughout the lesson sequence • Observations • Informal • Formal • Remediate/Enrich	
REFLECT (Step 5: Reflect on student learning) • Effectiveness • Successes • Modification	
START AGAIN (Step 6: Set new high, worthwhile goals) • For these students, at this time, in this setting	

Appendix G
Twenty Tips from Component 4 Assessors

1. NEVER shrink/reduce evidence. It must be readable at 100% magnification.
2. Follow YOUR certificate's instructions regarding the PROFILE GROUP size and makeup. Most certificates require a WHOLE CLASS.
3. Dig deep into the Knowledge of Students (KOS). Go beyond demographics. Your KOS NB Standard has many ideas.
4. Give specific data. If you say you collected data from a source, specifically describe that data and what you learned about your students from that data.
5. Know the NB definitions and purposes of Formative, Summative, and Student Self-Assessments. Particularly be aware of the *timing* of each within the component. Read the Portfolio Related Terms in the GENERAL Portfolio Instructions.
6. Be sure to address the IMPACT on student learning of your Professional Learning Need and in the Student Need. Use evidence that backs up your claims of impact.
7. Follow the page counts within the files you submit—don't go over! Do not alter forms in any way.
8. Choose a PLN and SN that have been fully implemented—otherwise it's not a good choice.
9. If your PLN and SN are related to each other, you cannot use the same evidence for both. The PLN is about your LEARNING. The SN is about COLLABORATION, etc. The evidence must match the need.
10. Strong PLN evidence goes beyond a PD certificate. Choose evidence that shows notes, agendas, or other data that shows YOUR learning.
11. Begin planning and collecting evidence for the PLN and SN early in the year so you have time to implement your plans and gather data.

12. The PLN and SN are about GROUPS, not individuals. If you teach ONLY 1:1, state that in your writing/on the forms.

13. Email evidence should have substance about the need—beyond "Let's meet." or "Thanks for the meeting." For example, a SN email might address collaboration or advocacy & its impact.

14. Do not waste character space listing the Standards or using phrases such as *As an accomplished teacher, I* ___. Use your space for specific evidence and rationales.

15. Submit only one version of the FA or SA—do not submit multiple versions. You can briefly explain if you used different versions. It's okay to submit different forms of the Student Self-Assessment.

16. The PLN and/or the SN CAN be about your Profile Group or can be about a different group.

17. Although it's not a hard and fast rule, answering the prompts in the order given is most helpful to the assessors. This writing is not a narrative telling a story.

18. Answer the prompts on forms with specificity.

19. Check formatting: double space the Written Commentary. It's okay to have a page of evidence in landscape format (assessors can flip them), but use portrait for all other writing.

20. FOLLOW DIRECTIONS, FOLLOW DIRECTIONS!

Appendix H
Component 4 Section Connections

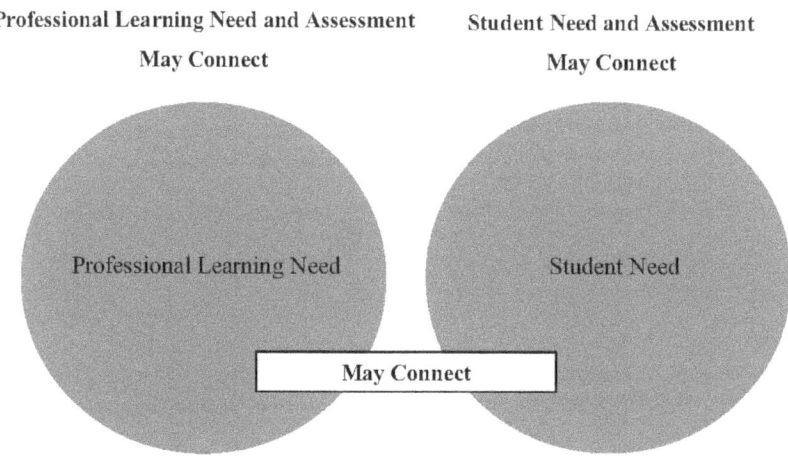

Figure H.1. Component 4 section connections. Created by author.

About the Author

Bobbie Faulkner spent thirty-eight years teaching grades K-6 in public schools in Ohio, Kentucky, and Arizona. She is a certified Middle Childhood Generalist and has renewed her certification. She has supported candidates in all certifications areas for almost two decades, and she has mentored candidates in her home district and state as well as in university and regional cohorts. She offers webinars to districts and cohorts on National Board topics. Bobbie can be contacted at nbwhatworks@gmail.com.